SECRETS

OF BLACK

HOLES

THE UNIVERSE'S MASTER BUILDERS

RAJEEV RAGHURAM

FriesenPress

One Printers Way
Altona, MB R0G 0B0
Canada

www.friesenpress.com

ISBN
978-1-03-914971-7 (Hardcover)
978-1-03-914970-0 (Paperback)
978-1-03-914972-4 (eBook).

1. JUVENILE NONFICTION, SCIENCE & NATURE, ASTRONOMY

Distributed to the trade by The Ingram Book Company

Table of Contents

Acknowledgements

Many thanks to my parents for giving me the utmost support and motivation to write this book.

I credit my physics teacher, Sarah Burnett, and the wonderful team of scientists from the documentary series "How the Universe Works" for providing me the basic knowledge and insight to write about a topic as fascinating as black holes.

And most importantly, I thank each and every one of my readers, because sharing my passion with the world will allow me to foster a new generation of astronomers.

Sagittarius A*, the supermassive black hole at the center of the Milky Way, was photographed for the first time by the Event Horizon telescope in May 2022.

Introduction

Decades ago, black holes were no more than science fiction. Nowadays, they are central to our understanding of the universe's evolution. They may seem intimidating and detrimental since nothing can escape from inside. However, the most basic property of black holes has led to many popular misconceptions regarding how they work, which prompts us, being human, to question why that is.

Although they can destroy stars and planets, black holes can also be creative forces in their environments. Galaxy evolution, and therefore the evolution of solar systems, are dependent on the complex processes driven by these perplexing objects. So you can think of them as destructive, but we owe them our very existence.

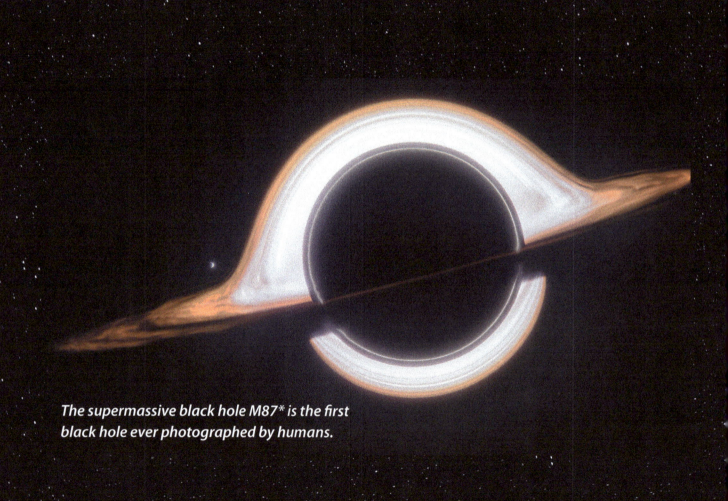

The supermassive black hole M87* is the first black hole ever photographed by humans.

Black Hole Basics

In order to understand how black holes can influence the universe around them, we must start with how they are scientifically measured. Black holes are measured in *solar masses*, since they are usually multiple times the mass of our Sun.

We have several categories of black holes based on their masses. *Stellar mass black holes*, which form from the deaths of massive stars, range from 3 to 100 solar masses. Supermassive black holes, which are studied the most intensively, can be millions or billions of times the mass of the Sun, and typically exist at the centers of galaxies. Even rarer are *ultramassive black holes*, which weigh more than 10 billion solar masses. Such monsters exist in the cores of the largest galaxies, or occasionally alone.

No matter how much mass a black hole has, they all have the same basic properties: they do not emit any light, and nothing can escape once inside. To effectively explain these properties, we need to look at them from the perspective of general relativity, which predicted the very existence of black holes in the first place.

The Sun bends spacetime more than the Earth due to its higher mass, and since its gravitational well is deeper, the Earth orbits around it.

Fundamentals of Spacetime

Albert Einstein's famous theory of general relativity is our most concrete theory to explain the universe we see today. It has taught us that space and time together create the most fundamental construct that exists, known as *spacetime*.

The concept of spacetime originates from Einstein's idea that the 3-dimensional universe we live in is intertwined with time itself, creating a 4-dimensional fabric in which all matter and energy is embedded. If spacetime were modeled as a flat sheet, objects with mass would distort and curve the fabric, just as a ball would warp the shape of the sheet.

The force we call gravity is really the curvature of spacetime. The more mass an object has, the deeper its gravitational well. This curvature dictates how matter moves through space, which explains why lower mass objects generally orbit around higher mass objects, and why objects with similar masses orbit each other.

Additionally, the density of an object determines how sharp the curvature is, causing the *strength* of gravitational attraction to vary at different distances from the object. If an object has a high mass in a small volume, there is a shorter distance between its center, where space is curved the most, and its farthest gravitational influence, where space is curved the least. As a result, a mass can be stretched in either direction, creating the forces we observe as tides.

Importantly, since space and time are linked to one another, a gravitational distortion of space also affects the flow of time. Deep inside the gravitational well of an object, time appears to run more slowly than farther away from that object or in zero gravity. This concept, known as *gravitational time dilation*, contradicts our original assumption that everyone experiences time at the same rate.

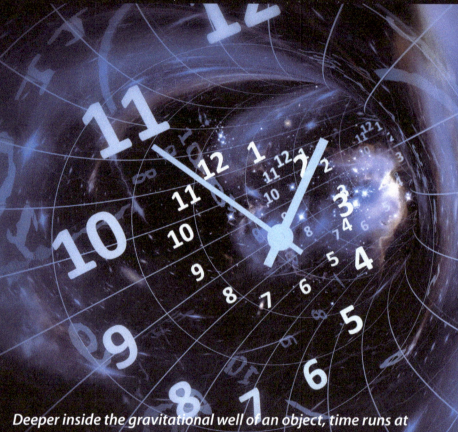

Deeper inside the gravitational well of an object, time runs at a slower rate relative to an outside observer.

For example, time runs slower on the surface of the Earth than in space above the planet. The time difference is just a fraction of a second, but satellites in low-Earth orbit are equipped with very precise atomic clocks that can measure these distinct time differences. The effectiveness of the Earth's GPS system completely relies on precision timing, which would not be possible if satellites did not account for the time differences between Earth's surface and in orbit.

However, since motion through space and time is *relative* to an outside observer, a traveler would not notice any differences with themselves or their immediate surroundings. This is an important consideration when applying principles of relativity to black holes, which show us the extremities of relativistic properties.

A black hole, just like any object with mass, creates curves in spacetime. However, black holes warp space to such an extent that at a certain distance from the center, known as the *event horizon,* the escape velocity equals the speed of light. The event horizon is also the point where time stops moving, due to gravitational time dilation, but most importantly, it is the point of no return, since anything inside would have to travel faster than light to escape.

Because of *relative velocity time dilation,* it is impossible for anything to travel through space faster than the speed of light. Since space and time are linked, any object is always moving. Even an object that appears stationary is still moving, but it is only moving through time.

A stationary object moves through time at the fastest possible rate. However, when an object starts moving, some of its motion through time converts into motion through space. As a result, the object would be moving slower through time relative to an outside observer. If the object were to reach the speed of light, which is a universal constant, it would be moving through space *only*, and its time will have stopped relative to the observer.

Because of time dilation, something moving faster than the speed of light would move backwards in time to maintain the constant rate of motion through spacetime. If this happened, this would violate Einstein's principle of causality, which explains the simple cause-and-effect scenarios we see in our daily lives. This supposed violation of the causality principle tells us that nothing can travel through space faster than the speed of light.

Due to gravitational lensing, the light from the flares was bent around the black hole so that we could observe it.

The event horizon can be thought of as the "surface" of a black hole, because deeper than this point, the escape velocity surpasses the speed of light, the universe's speed limit, so nothing can get out. As a result, they do not emit light, so they appear "black". However, just outside the event horizon, the dynamics of spacetime can create wonders.

Due to gravitational time dilation, traveling close to the event horizon causes the traveler's clock to move slower relative to Earth. Since the traveler would experience less time than an observer on Earth, they would have moved into the observer's future, which would be a real-life example of time travel. However, another important consideration is how the gravity of the black hole affects space.

Since all light is embedded in spacetime itself, its path is directly affected by the geometry of spacetime. Around a black hole, we typically see huge rings of light above the event horizon. This distortion is caused by the black hole's curvature of spacetime, which we know as gravity. Beams of light from faraway objects, such as stars, follow these curves and get bent around the black hole before coming into view. This effect is known as *gravitational lensing*, and it can bend the light to form beautiful arcs and circles.

In August 2021, scientists got a glimpse into the lensing effect by studying X-ray flares from the galaxy I Zwicky 1, located 59 million light years from Earth. The flares appeared to originate from turbulent material surrounding the supermassive black hole at the galaxy's center. They occurred on the other side of the black hole from our view, but due to the gravitational lensing of the black hole, the light from the flares was bent into view and was detected on Earth by the Nuclear Spectroscopic Telescope Array (NuSTAR) and the XMM-Newton space telescope, which are designed to observe X-ray wavelengths of light.

While all black holes have the same relativistic properties and exemplify gravitational lensing, they can all form in different ways. This allows us to begin to answer the question as to how exactly black holes shape the universe around us.

The star's core only collapses into a black hole after the star explodes, allowing the light and matter from the supernova to escape.

The Birth of Black Holes

Black holes have shaped the entire universe throughout cosmic history, but it all starts with their formation. The simplest way of forming a stellar mass black hole is from the death of a star. A star that is at least 8 times the mass of the Sun will live a short life – no more than 100 million years – and explode as a *supernova*.

If the star's core weighs between 1.4 and 2.2 solar masses, it will collapse to form a *neutron star*, one of the densest and fastest spinning objects in the universe. Nonetheless, the star can still support its own weight since it is made predominantly of neutrons. According to the Pauli Exclusion Principle in quantum mechanics, no two neutrons can occupy identical quantum states at the same time and will instead fill the lowest available energy state present in the system. As a result, neutrons will naturally repel each other with extreme force, an effect known as *neutron degeneracy pressure*. The outward pressure is strong enough to counteract the gravitational contraction of the neutron star, so it cannot collapse further.

However, if the core weighs more than about 3 solar masses, its gravity becomes strong enough to overcome the outward force of neutron degeneracy pressure and continue collapsing. As a result, the core collapses as far as it will go, forming a stellar mass black hole. Because of this minimum mass needed for the core collapse, stellar mass black holes only form from stars at least 20 times the mass of the Sun.

An alternative method of forming a stellar mass black hole is an *unnova*, a failed supernova. In the galaxy NGC 6946, nicknamed the "Fireworks Galaxy" due to the high frequency of supernovas observed there, scientists witnessed a 25-solar-mass star named N6946-BH1 just blink out, evidence that it underwent an unnova.

In theory, heavy elements would accumulate on the surface of the core. When the star collapses, the outer layers would normally "bounce" upon striking the core. As energy is transferred to the layers of lighter elements, the immense pressure would generate a shockwave that tears through the surrounding material and creates the explosion.

However, in an unnova, the gravitational collapse is strong enough to prevent the shockwave from reaching the surface. As a result, the supernova "fails" and the material collapses into a stellar mass black hole. Since there was no explosion, and therefore no mass ejected, the black hole would have the entire mass of the progenitor star.

In the case of N6946-BH1, scientists were able to confirm that an unnova had occurred by studying light on the infrared portion of the electromagnetic spectrum. Astronomers detected a distinct flow of infrared light coming from the same location as the star was originally, and they thought that surrounding material fell into the black hole left over from the failed supernova, generating infrared light that we could observe. Based on these results, as well as observations of other stars, we now believe that 10 to 30 percent of giant stars could die as unnovae, leaving behind stellar mass black holes.

Since intermediate mass black holes require unique conditions to form, they appear to be much rarer than other types of black holes.

Since we have observed stellar mass black holes, as well as giant black holes, it is natural to question why we have not observed a black hole in between these two mass ranges. This mysterious type of black hole, known as the *intermediate mass black hole*, would be between 100 and 100,000 solar masses. However, since they are too large to form from the deaths of stars, the mechanisms by which they are created are somewhat unclear.

Nevertheless, on May 21, 2019, the Laser Interferometer Gravitational-Wave Observatory (LIGO) found direct evidence for the existence of intermediate black holes. It detected a signal of *gravitational waves,* ripples in the fabric of spacetime, that were created by the collision of two stellar black holes. One weighed roughly 66 solar masses, and the other was 85 solar masses. The data suggested that the final black hole was about 142 times the Sun's mass, confirmation of the first intermediate mass black hole ever discovered.

While we only have one confirmed discovery of an intermediate black hole, astronomers predict that they could be relatively common in today's universe. For example, the globular star cluster 47 Tucanae is held together by a central object invisible to telescopes, and scientists were able to calculate its mass by measuring the orbital speeds of multiple pulsars, neutron stars that emit flashing beams of radiation from their poles. The math reveals that the object must have roughly 2,000 solar masses, and since we cannot see it directly, it is most likely an intermediate mass black hole.

We know that intermediate mass black holes can form from the merger of two smaller black holes, but another theory states that they could also form straight from a cloud of gas. This would be most feasible in the early universe, where hydrogen and helium gas were the most prevalent. As a result, clouds would be much denser and more prone to collapse.

However, direct collapse requires very precise conditions. A cold gas cloud typically has an uneven spread of density, causing it to fragment into multiple stars. For the cloud to collapse into a single object, it must be perfectly symmetrical, which means that it must retain a certain amount of energy as it collapses. For example, the turbulence created by nearby star formation could inject enough energy into the cloud to prevent it from fragmenting, which would allow it to directly collapse into an intermediate mass black hole.

As for supermassive and ultramassive black holes, there may be no single mechanism of creating them. Physicists believe that there was not enough time since the birth of the universe for small black holes to grow so large, so multiple methods might be needed. In order to solve these mysteries, we have to start with understanding the mechanism by which all black holes can grow, consuming the matter around them.

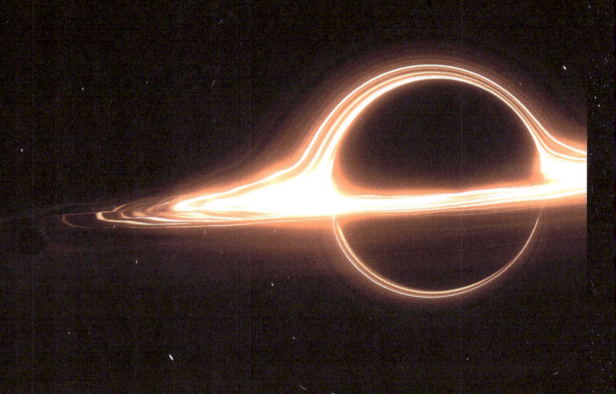

Up to 40 percent of the matter in the accretion disk gets converted to energy, making it shine brighter than an entire galaxy.

A Whirlpool of Spacetime

When we study black holes and the effects on their ambient surroundings, we notice that they are typically surrounded by a brightly glowing ring. This ring of material, known as the *accretion disk*, feeds the black hole around which it orbits. But, more importantly, the black hole's interaction with the disk can reveal the complex processes occurring in the vicinity, as well as some physical properties of the black hole.

An accretion disk only forms around a rotating black hole, known as a *Kerr black hole*, due to the black hole's interaction with the spacetime around it. A non-rotating black hole, known as a *Schwarzschild black hole*, cannot easily form an accretion disk. Inside the event horizon, where the escape velocity is greater than the speed of light, spacetime flows directly towards the center of the black hole, like water down a waterfall. However, outside the event horizon, the black hole's rotation causes the space around it to spin as well, just as the eye of a hurricane causes the surrounding air to swirl around it.

This rotation is known in general relativity as *frame dragging*, which occurs with any massive object with spin. The more massive the object and the faster it spins, the greater the effect. Due to the swirling movement of spacetime, the initially unimpeded trajectory of a moving object would be dragged in the direction of the rotation of the spinning object.

Frame dragging is what leads to the formation of the accretion disk. The black hole's gravity attracts nearby gas and dust, which embeds in the spacetime surrounding the black hole. This space, which already has the whirlpool motion due to the spin of the black hole, carries the material with it. Since the gas is being dragged by the spinning spacetime, and it also has its own angular momentum through space, the material orbits the black hole at a considerable fraction of the speed of light. The rapid rotation causes the matter to flatten into a Saturn-like ring, which becomes the accretion disk.

While the disk may seem like an ordinary feature, it is the most efficient way for a black hole to feed on surrounding material. The common misconception is that black holes will eat everything that surrounds them, but the physics of spacetime states that this is not entirely true. Gravity is directly proportional to the distortion of spacetime by an object with mass, which in turn is directly proportional to the object's mass. As a result, the gravity of a stellar mass black hole, for example, would be the same as a star with the same amount of mass. Additionally, due to the frame dragging of spacetime, matter cannot fall into the black hole from any direction. Instead, it would have to orbit close enough to enter.

One of the characteristic properties of the accretion disk is the extremely high energy emitted. Since matter in the disk can have a dispersion of velocities, the particles would frequently collide or grind past each other, generating intense friction. The force of friction generates heat, and the stronger the friction, the hotter the system gets. In this case, the disk spins at a significant fraction of the speed of light, so the frictional forces heat the gas to millions of degrees. The thermal vibration of the particles is converted into high-energy radiation, which allows us to observe the system here on Earth.

While the black hole gives off no light, the accretion disk can be billions of times brighter than the Sun. This severe contrast creates a "shadow" that allows us to photograph the black hole. The way we observe the black hole depends on the orientation of the accretion disk relative to Earth. If we see the disk edge-on, the black hole would be obscured by hot gas, and hence hidden by a halo of light. However, in some cases, the disk is tilted precisely into our line of sight, so we directly see the silhouette of the black hole. When scientists used the Event Horizon telescope to make such observations, they captured perhaps the most revolutionary image in the history of astrophysics.

At the center of the Messier 87 (M87) galaxy, 55 million light years away, lies the black hole in question. This monster, known as M87*, is the first black hole ever imaged. While the bright accretion disk allows us to photograph the supermassive black hole itself, it also reveals some of the black hole's important physical properties.

For example, the luminosity of the disk can be used to calculate the mass of the black hole, because more mass and more gravity led to more material piling up in the disk, and therefore a higher energy output. In the case of M87*, scientists determined that it has roughly 6.5 billion solar masses. Additionally, recalibrating the sensors allows us to see different wavelengths of light emitted by the disk, which reveal other processes powered by the black hole.

M87* in regular light (left) and polarized light (right). The patterns of polarized light are the signature of magnetic fields around the black hole.

While the first image of M87* was released in 2019, scientists released a new image in 2021 that showed its accretion disk in polarized light, evidence for the presence of magnetic fields in the black hole's vicinity. We think these magnetic fields originate from the extreme heat of the accretion disk. When the gas is heated to millions of degrees, electrons are forced to break their electromagnetic bonds with atomic nuclei and fly around freely. As a result, the disk is mostly plasma, consisting of individual charged particles.

According to the laws of particle physics, a charged subatomic particle has an associated electric field surrounding it, which allows it to attract oppositely charged particles. However, when a particle moves, its electric field moves with it, which creates a magnetic field. The high concentration of plasma in the accretion disk creates a strong magnetic field that naturally orients itself along the black hole's axis of rotation. As a result, the magnetic poles of the disk line up with the black hole's axial poles.

Remember that a charged particle has an associated electric field, and that a moving electric field generates a magnetic field. Since magnetic fields can attract each other, charged particles in the accretion disk would be captured and circulated around the vicinity by the rapidly spinning magnetic fields of the black hole.

When charged particles get trapped in the magnetic fields, light emitted from the accretion disk would undergo polarization, which is dictated by the rules of quantum electrodynamics. Since light is created by subatomic particles in the form of electromagnetic waves, a photon is really an oscillating electric field coupled with a magnetic field, which constitute a cumulative electromagnetic field. If this field oscillates in the same direction as the photon travels, we say that the photon has linear polarization. A photon with circular or elliptical polarization has the field oscillating in a plane parallel to the photon's direction of travel.

Normally, we observe light as being unpolarized since all of its photons have an equal distribution of polarizations. Unpolarized light can become polarized if it passes through a polarizer, which absorbs or reflects all photons that do not have a specific polarization. For example, the chemical laminate pattern that makes up the lenses of sunglasses acts as a polarizer that filters the light so that only the photons with circular polarization become visible.

We typically use polarizers that either absorb or reflect light, but they typically require matter that has a certain structure. However, with the inclusion of a magnetic field component, light becomes polarized via the Faraday effect. The magnetic field component causes the photon's plane of polarization to rotate in a circle. As a result, the photon's polarization becomes circular.

In the case of M87*, charged dust particles are trapped in the magnetic fields surrounding the supermassive black hole, filtering the light so that we only detect the photons with circular polarization. By measuring the distinct spiral pattern of polarized light in the image, we can track the movement of the dust particles which are responsible for polarizing the light. This allows us to map out the magnetic fields around the black hole.

Studying the polarized light from M87* gives us insights into the way magnetic fields affect how fast the black hole eats. The fields could slow down the rapidly orbiting plasma and allow it to fall into the black hole, accelerating its growth. Alternatively, the fields could push away gas, reducing the rate at which the black hole feeds.

These two possibilities suggest that magnetism plays an important role in regulating M87*'s growth, and other disturbances in its environment could provide more food for the supermassive black hole. However, when a black hole eats too much, its growth can suddenly be halted by huge bursts of energy, which can be seen clear across the universe.

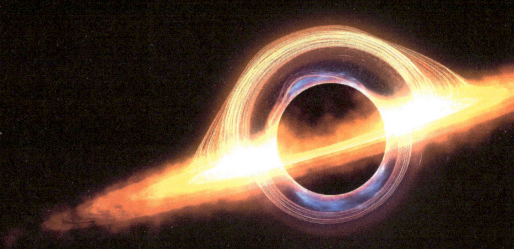

The light pressure in the accretion disk superheats the surrounding gas, creating winds that blow away from the black hole at a quarter of the speed of light.

Cosmic Outbursts

Black holes may appear to be simple: the more matter they consume, the bigger and more massive they get. However, black holes can easily be described as messy eaters, because they sometimes eat too much, and the excess food can be ejected violently. This creates some of the brightest flares in the universe.

In order to understand the physics behind these phenomena, we must start with the way a black hole grows. Gas from the surroundings is dragged into its accretion disk, which heats up as it spins faster and faster. The immense heat causes the system to radiate light, primarily in the ultraviolet. If the black hole is "calm," or eating at a relatively low rate, it will generate a steady flow of light.

However, when a black hole eats faster than normal, more material piles up in the accretion disk, raising pressures and temperatures. When the disk reaches a certain temperature, it will start to emit X-rays, which can create a powerful but less noticeable effect called a black hole wind.

The high-energy X-rays emitted by the disk energize clouds of gas and dust surrounding the black hole. A hot gas must increase in volume in order to maintain a constant pressure, so the superheated gas rapidly expands outwards. Since the winds consist of material around the black hole, and the X-ray light that generates them is emitted in all directions, the wind blows outward in a spherical shell. As a result, the winds may appear to be simple, but a new study suggests that the wind experiences a cycle of regular temperature changes.

The NuSTAR and XMM-Newton space telescopes study the dynamics of the wind by taking spectra of its light. Certain heavy elements present in the winds, such as iron, absorb specific wavelengths of light. This absorption shows up in the spectrum as distinct holes, known as absorption features, and we can determine the overall elemental composition of the wind based on these patterns.

Eventually, scientists observed that the absorption features repeatedly appeared and disappeared from the spectra. When the gas absorbs the light, its temperature rises continuously until it becomes completely saturated with X-rays, at which point it cannot absorb any more. As a result, the wind radiates away this light and cools off, allowing for more X-rays to be absorbed and the absorption features to appear in the spectra once again. If the black hole is actively feeding, the cycle will constantly repeat.

While the black hole's winds may seem subtle, they can have a profound effect on the evolution of the galaxy around it. Stars form from dense clouds of cold hydrogen gas, which is abundant in most galaxies. However, the winds heat up the gas, preventing it from collapsing to form stars. The gas expands as it heats up, so its density decreases. Eventually, as the gas gets pushed away and becomes less dense, it can no longer form stars. As a result, the winds can shut down star formation over the long term, a process known as *quenching*.

We typically observe quenched star birth in massive elliptical galaxies, which have a spherical or ovular distribution of stars. Elliptical galaxies generally contain old red stars, because they have not formed new stars in billions of years. After these stars first formed, the gas from which they formed started to feed the supermassive black hole at the core of the young galaxy. The black hole began to generate winds, which blew away the vital star-forming gas that was abundant in the galaxy. As a result, star formation ceased, leaving only red dwarf stars and giving the galaxy a monotone color. Since black hole winds expand as a sphere, and elliptical galaxies are usually a similar shape, ellipticals are most vulnerable to wind-based quenching.

In contrast, spiral galaxies like the Milky Way are safer from this effect because their structure differs greatly from ellipticals. The galaxy consists of spiral arms, which are almost perfectly flat, surrounding a central bulge, which is normally spherical. However, instead of being spherical, the Milky Way's central bulge mainly consists of stars that have extremely elongated orbits, resembling the shape of a bar. Such galaxies are called barred spirals.

The Milky Way's galactic bar was measured to be 27,000 light years long, but more importantly, it appears to only contain red stars. This suggests that the central regions of the galaxy are under the influence of black hole winds.

Although the spiral arms of the Milky Way contain mostly young stars, star birth has been quenched in the galactic core due to Sagittarius A*'s winds.

The supermassive black hole at the center of our galaxy, Sagittarius A*, weighs roughly 4 million solar masses. Today, it does not appear to be actively feeding. However, this black hole must have fed on gas several times in the past to grow to its current size. With each meal, winds from the black hole blew away matter present in the galaxy's heart, shutting down star formation. Furthermore, the galactic bar can funnel material toward the super-massive black hole, intensifying the winds and accelerating the quenching process.

When Sagittarius A* used up its entire food supply, the winds subsided, and the black hole returned to being quiescent. But the presence of only red stars in the galactic bar highlights the impact of feeding events on the black hole's local environment. Another important con-sideration is that the Milky Way's spiral arms are replete with stars of all different colors.

Depending on the star's temperature, it emits certain wavelengths of light, which we per-ceive as colors. If the star is hotter, the light it emits have a shorter wavelength, but a higher energy. As a result, the light will shift toward the blue end of the spectrum. Stars hotter than the Sun appear blue or white, and cooler stars appear orange or red.

The larger the star is, the hotter its core becomes. This speeds up the rate of nuclear fusion reactions, so it burns through its fuel faster and has a shorter lifespan. As a result, we can generalize that the bright blue stars that we observe in a galaxy are younger, since they live very short lives and die quickly. If these stars are young, the gas clouds from which they form existed recently, so a supermassive black hole's winds have not had enough time to quench star formation in that galaxy.

The spiral arms of a galaxy can host active star formation although the galaxy's nucleus appears much older. However, if black hole winds could propagate throughout an entire spiral galaxy, the spiral arms would appear just as old as the core. The relative structures of the spiral arms and central bulge are the key in understanding how quenching has less impact on spiral galaxies.

While the central bulge is generally spherical, the spiral arms are almost perfectly flat. Since winds from the supermassive black hole expand spherically, they do not directly flow into the spiral arms. Additionally, the gas clouds from which stars form are unevenly dis-tributed throughout the galaxy, so the winds will not always expand into one. In the end, the winds would only inject a small amount of energy into star-forming clouds, while the rest would exit the galaxy altogether. As a result, star formation in the galaxy would be largely undisturbed.

While the winds can affect a galaxy over the long term, a supermassive black hole can create much more energetic outbursts that can have direct effects on the surroundings. In September 2019, astronomers witnessed a bright flare coming from a spiral galaxy 215 million light years away. The flash was evidence of a tidal disruption event, where a super-massive black hole feasted on a closely orbiting star. Named AT2019qiz, this was the closest such event ever recorded.

The data suggests that the consumed star was roughly the same mass as the Sun, while the supermassive black hole weighed about a million solar masses. Because of the huge differ-ence in masses, the star got ripped apart by the enormous tidal forces of the black hole.

We can explain the star's fatal encounter using the physics of gravity. Normally, we say that the object is in a gravitationally bound state. However, the object would need to absorb a certain amount of energy to cease being in this state. The minimum amount of energy needed for the object to exit the gravitationally bound state, or "fall apart", is the object's gravitational binding energy.

The supermassive black hole in AT2019qiz snares trails of stellar debris, which violently collide with the accretion disk to produce the flares.

In the AT2019qiz system, the supermassive black hole exerted a gravitational force on the star that was many times greater than the star's gravitational binding energy. As a result, the star was unable to hold itself together and got shredded by the gravity of the black hole.

As the black hole rotates, the star gets stretched a huge looping stream of gas. It also experiences relativistic precession as it orbits the black hole, meaning that its trajectory shifts slightly with each orbit. With enough orbits, the star's path appears to follow the shape of a flower. However, when the debris follows this path, it can start to self-intersect. When the orbiting material collides with itself, it releases energy into the surroundings and sinks closer to the black hole, where it can be gobbled up.

The release of energy creates a luminous flare, which was detected in ultraviolet light, X-rays, visible light, and radio waves. This burst of radiation pushes infalling material back outward at 10,000 kilometers per second, partially blocking the light coming from the accretion disk. By studying the light behind the ejecta, astronomers can more accurately determine the origin and distribution of gas surrounding the black hole.

However, winds and flares are not the only violent effects created by an actively feeding black hole. It will attract anything that gets too close. If a black hole were to gorge on matter fast enough, it could generate a powerful "burp" that would hot only wreak havoc on its local environment, but on the entire galaxy.

These violent outbursts arise from magnetic activity within the accretion disk. As the black hole spins, the magnetic fields of the disk intensify and start to capture plasma particles. The field is wound up tightly by the spin of the black hole as the particles are funneled to the poles, building up magnetic energy as they accumulate.

But as more and more particles get trapped, the magnetic fields eventually become completely saturated, at which point they can no longer contain their stored energy. When this happens, the field snaps and blasts out twin jets of high-energy radiation. We used to believe that the extreme energy comes from the base of the jet, but spectroscopic analysis suggests that more complex systems are in action to create the energies we observe in the jets.

We have observed that if the black hole does not have jets, the light from the system is mainly ultraviolet light from the accretion disk. However, black holes with jets are far brighter in X-rays. This distinction can be explained by the presence of a corona. Like the Sun's corona, it is a layer of hot, diffuse gas that forms a spherical shell around the black hole. Due to the extreme heat, the black hole's corona also generates strong magnetic fields.

When the jets strike the intergalactic medium, the diffuse layer of gas between the galaxies, the gas spreads out spherically to form the Fermi bubbles.

When the magnetic poles of the black hole become oversaturated with particles and radiation, the particles are launched outward in narrow beams. However, if the jets were simply powered by the magnetic fields threaded around the black hole, they would produce far less energy and travel far slower than what we have observed. The jets must be amplified and accelerated by a system other than the black hole's magnetic field. The web of magnetic fields in the black hole's corona checks both boxes.

When photons in the jets enter the corona, they can ricochet off plasma particles and gain energy. As a result, ultraviolet photons can be converted to X-rays, and the highest energy X-rays can become gamma rays. Additionally, the high-speed charged particles get further accelerated as they are redirected by the magnetic fields. Once the jets pass through the corona, they travel at close to the speed of light and are ablaze with X-rays and gamma rays.

Recently, NASA's Chandra X-ray observatory has studied jets coming from M87*, the supermassive black hole that was photographed in 2019. Chandra has measured M87*'s jets to be roughly 18,000 light years long, but interestingly, the X-ray data suggests that the jets are not a single structure. Instead, they consist of multiple distinct knots that push up against each other as they propagate through space. These knots are created when matter falls into the black hole at different rates, creating streams of X-ray light that are distinctly brighter or dimmer than others.

Between 2012 and 2017, scientists tracked the movement of two knots in order to accurately measure their velocity. One is 900 light years from M87*, while the other is 2,500 light years away from the supermassive black hole. However, the farther knot appears to be travelling at 2.4 times the speed of light, while the closer one appears to move at 6.3 times the speed of light. This surprising result may seem to violate causality, but this is an example of superluminal motion.

The jets are travelling at almost the same speed as the light inside them. If the jet is pointed directly toward an observer, they would have the illusion that the overall motion of the jet is faster than light. On Earth, we see the jets almost directly face-on, so the *apparent* velocities were faster than light. Later, Chandra accurately measured the speed of the jets, and found that they travel at 99 percent the speed of light, which does not violate any physics.

Since the jets have such a high energy density and velocity, they can cause mass chaos in the black hole's host galaxy. For example, we have observed two vast lobes of gas above and below the plane of the Milky Way known as the Fermi bubbles. To find out their origin, scientists have traced the bubbles to the center of our galaxy, where Sagittarius A* resides.

Roughly 6 million years ago, Sagittarius A* must have eaten a huge meal, perhaps a group of wayward stars. This sudden jolt of inflowing energy triggered a huge cosmic burp, unleashing powerful jets that blew out across hundreds of thousands of light years. When the jets struck cold gas surrounding the supermassive black hole, they unleashed massive shockwaves. These shockwaves caused the gas to puff out into huge clouds, which formed the Fermi bubbles that we see today.

Jets are fueled by cold gas, but during a feeding event, the gas is either blown away or consumed by the black hole. So, after about a million years, Sagittarius A*'s jets switched off as it finished its meal, and the supermassive black hole returned to being calm. While the Fermi bubbles may look beautiful, they are scars concealing the black hole's violent past.

Most of the time, the jets do not create such beauty. They can tear huge holes in gas clouds known as voids. In the galaxy NGC 2276, located 100 million light years from Earth, scientists observed a massive void in one of the galaxy's spiral arms, where young stars should be forming. However, the detection of a burst of X-rays and radio waves indicates the presence of a mysterious object in the center of this cavity. Based on the X-ray and radio luminosities, scientists concluded that the object, named NGC2276-3c, is likely an intermediate mass black hole with an estimated mass of 50,000 solar masses.

It is possible that NGC2276-3c could be the leftover core of a dwarf galaxy that merged with NGC 2276. As the black hole sunk into one of the galaxy's spiral arms, it would have swallowed up gas clouds and disrupted the orbits of nearby stars, forming a void. Additionally, the black hole appeared to eat too much and launched jets, which travelled up to 2,000 light years in either direction. We have observed that the 1,000-light-year radius surrounding the black hole is devoid of young stars, which makes sense, because the gas clouds in this region were superheated and pushed away.

However, since the jets run on cold gas, they eventually shut down as the gas is blown away. Additionally, this material is the food source for the black hole, so when the jets turn off, the black hole stops growing. The black hole will eventually attract more gas and feed once again as it orbits the core of the galaxy. While jets and winds from black holes may seem to be ordinary processes in contemporary galaxies, they could potentially explain one of the most important evolutionary transitions in the history of the universe.

Discovering huge populations
of supermassive black holes
in the early universe is mysterious,
since even stars were still somewhat
rare at that time.

The Dark Ages

The farther we look into the universe, the farther back in time we are looking, because light takes time to traverse the cosmos. We see distant galaxies as they were billions of years ago, not as they are today. However, we see that roughly a billion years after the Big Bang, the universe went from dark to light. One of the biggest questions in cosmology is what force drove this transformation. To begin to answer it, we must look back to the very beginning of the universe.

13.8 billion years ago, the universe burst into life. During the first second of the Big Bang, the fundamental building blocks of the universe – space, time, matter, and energy – were created and set in motion. As the infant universe expanded and cooled, energy converted into matter, according to Einstein's equation $E=mc^2$. 380,000 years later, the energies decreased enough for subatomic particles to cluster together. The first atoms formed, releasing the light we see today as the cosmic microwave background, the oldest light we can observe.

As more and more atoms continued to form, they built up huge clouds of hydrogen and helium gas. At this time, the universe is still shining brightly, but as space continued to expand, the energy diminished further. Eventually, the universe, covered in fog, became completely dark. This period is known as the Dark Ages.

The universe eventually became bright again during the Epoch of Reionization, where new light was created, and the primordial gas clouds started to clear. However, although the reionization of the universe was likely caused by the birth of the first stars, we are not yet certain. One intriguing idea is that supermassive black holes could be partially responsible for the reionization process.

On January 12, 2021, astronomers announced that they have discovered a huge supermassive black hole over 13 billion light years away. This object, named J0313-1806, is the oldest and most distant supermassive black hole ever discovered. It existed just 670 million years after the Big Bang, but shockingly, it weighs over 1.6 billion solar masses.

This black hole is currently a *quasar,* meaning that it is actively feeding. Quasars are the brightest objects in the universe and can be seen from billions of light years away. Unlike a feeding black hole's occasional "burp", quasars are fueled by galaxy-sized quantities of matter and can be sustained for millions of years at a time, generating much more energy. J0313-1806 shines 1,000 times brighter than all the stars in the Milky Way combined. As a result, it, along with a population of other supermassive black holes in the early universe, may have helped the universe transition out of the Dark Ages.

When J0313-1806 initially formed, it still would have been shrouded in thick clouds of gas. However, as it began to eat and generate light, it would drive a quasar wind, which expands away from the supermassive black hole at 20 percent the speed of light. The wind would push gas away, creating an ionized pocket within the intergalactic medium. Additionally, quasars could also drive jets, which would further increase the size of the voids.

If the largest population III stars died as unnovae, they could have left behind "seed" black holes that gradually became supermassive.

Since stars are small and their stellar winds cannot propagate far, ionized pockets created by stars would be small. By contrast, quasars would create much larger holes, since their winds and jets can have strong influences beyond their immediate surroundings. We cannot yet directly measure the ionized pockets in the early universe to definitively say which objects helped end the Dark Ages, but it is possible that the first stars and black holes were both responsible, since they formed at around the same time.

But as we find more and more quasars in the early universe, an enduring mystery arises: how did these supermassive black holes get so big so quickly? They surely could not have formed from the deaths of the first stars. Instead, it seems reasonable that intermediate mass black holes could have served as "seeds" for the first supermassive black holes. To prove the theory, we need to understand how intermediate mass black holes can grow.

One interesting idea is that some intermediate black holes could have formed from exotic stars known as population III stars. Stars today have a size limit, which is determined by their composition. For context, the Sun is roughly 74 percent hydrogen and 25 percent helium by mass. However, the remaining 1 percent of the Sun's mass comprises heavier elements, such as oxygen, silicon, and iron. The composition of the star is shown by the frequencies of light in its spectrum.

We have observed that low-mass stars tend to have more heavy elements in them. This is an important consideration, because heavy elements trap heat inside the star, reducing the temperatures needed to initiate nuclear fusion reactions. The stars that have the fewest heavy elements are the most massive, which makes sense, because they require far more heat to spark fusion than lower mass stars.

Today, the largest star we know of is R136a1, which is 265 times the mass of the Sun. However, during the Dark Ages, the universe consisted entirely of hydrogen and helium gas. Since there were no heavy elements at this time, population III stars, which were the first generation of stars, had to be far larger to ignite fusion, and could be 1,000 times the mass of the Sun or more. They would be much hotter and brighter, and their composition of solely hydrogen and helium would yield unique spectra that would differ greatly from today's stars.

Due to their extreme mass, population III stars would be very short-lived and die after less than 10 million years. They most likely died as supernovae, which would spread heavy elements into nebulae that formed the next generation of stars. However, if the star dies as a supernova, most of its mass is ejected, leaving only a small amount of matter behind to form a black hole. Instead, some of these first-generation stars must have died as unnovae, which would form black holes weighing thousands of solar masses.

Dark matter at the cores of protogalaxies could have fed intermediate mass black holes directly or by drawing in visible matter.

Intermediate mass black holes could have formed from population III stars or from the direct collapse of the primordial gas clouds in the early universe. However, once the "seed" black hole forms, it still needs time to grow. It is unlikely that there was enough time since the Big Bang for these black holes to become supermassive just by eating matter around them, so other mechanisms are needed.

One creative idea is that intermediate black holes grew with the aid of *dark matter*, the most abundant and elusive form of matter in the universe. Dark matter does not interact with light, so we cannot observe it directly, but it has gravity and can affect visible matter. Our measurements suggest that 85 percent of all the matter in the universe is dark matter, and we now know that it has had a profound effect on the evolution of the universe.

Dark matter began to clump together in the early universe, creating regions of higher gravity. As a result, normal matter was dragged into these wells and collapsed to form the first stars, which would not be possible without the inclusion of dark matter. Similarly, dark matter wells could have pulled in enough gas to trigger direct collapse and form intermediate black holes. This could be much more efficient than a direct collapse caused by other disturbances.

Another possibility starts with a small galaxy forming around a growing intermediate mass black hole. This protogalaxy would likely be an elliptical, since it has not had time to flatten out into a disk, which would form a spiral galaxy. Since the core is the densest region of the galaxy, it would accumulate the most dark matter. As a result, the gravity of the dark matter could funnel material towards the intermediate mass black hole at the center, increasing its rate of growth.

While dark matter's gravity may assist with the growth of the first intermediate mass black holes, another important consideration is how magnetism shapes the development of galaxies. As a protogalaxy rotates, it flattens into a spiral shaped disk, compressing gas clouds and increasing the rate of star formation. Shockwaves from supernovas or black hole jets induce turbulence in galactic gas clouds. Charged particles in the clouds swirl around each other, generating powerful magnetic fields that extend far out into space.

Gradually, the magnetic fields in gas clouds throughout the disk start to envelop the entire galaxy. The magnetic fields that are distributed internally through the galaxy can channel gas particles in a certain direction, based on their orientation. Sometimes, the fields can direct gas towards the intermediate mass black hole at the core of the galaxy, which would also allow it to grow faster.

However, although the invisible forces of dark matter and magnetism can speed up the growth of early black holes, the simplest and most efficient mechanism would be for black holes to collide and merge with one another.

When black holes or neutron stars orbit each other,
they emit gravitational waves into their surroundings,
which gradually depletes their orbital energy until
they merge.

Cosmic Cannibalism

Scientists are striving to understand how supermassive black holes grew to the sizes that they are today. Since the growth of supermassive black holes is intricately linked to the evolution of their host galaxies, we have come up with some intriguing theories. The influence of dark matter and magnetic fields would partially explain this growth, but since black holes will eat everything, they will eat each other as well, which could be the most efficient mechanism by which they grow.

In order to understand how black holes can cannibalize one another, we need to begin to explore the realm of gravitational waves. Remember that any object with mass curves spacetime. Because of the gravitational attraction between objects, no object is truly static. A moving object creates ripples in the fabric of spacetime, just as a moving boat creates ripples on the surface of water.

These ripples, known as gravitational waves, are emitted when any object moves through space. The amplitude of the waves is a measure of their intensity, or how "loud" they are, while their frequency measures how often they are emitted. Amplitude is dependent on the mass of the object emitting the waves, while the rate at which the object is moving determines their frequency.

The advanced LIGO observatory is the most sensitive gravitational wave detection system on the planet. It consists of two separate detectors: one in Livingston, Louisiana, and the other in Hanford, Washington. Each detector consists of an interferometer, which diverts a laser beam into two paths that are each 4 kilometers (2.5 miles) in length. The beams reflect off mirrors at the end of the tunnel and converge at the point where they were split, where scientists can make measurements.

The two laser beams are normally the same length. However, a passing gravitational wave stretches and compresses spacetime, which increases the length of one arm and decreases the length of the other. The effect is extremely tiny, since the gravitational waves striking the beams are narrower than an atomic nucleus, but LIGO's sensors are powerful enough to detect this change. As a result, it, along with other gravitational wave detectors around the world, is revolutionizing astronomy.

On September 14, 2015, LIGO made history by making the first ever direct detection of gravitational waves. The data from this event, named GW150914, suggests that 1.3 billion years ago, two stellar mass black holes had violently collided. Based on the amplitude and frequency of the gravitational waves, scientists worked out that one of the black holes was 29 times the mass of the Sun, while the other was 36 times the mass of the Sun. When the two black holes finally collided and merged, the resulting black hole weighed 62 solar masses.

This result may seem controversial because the final black hole weighs 3 solar masses less than the sum of the masses of the two original black holes, which appears to violate the law of mass conservation. However, gravitational waves involved in the event can solve this mystery.

As the black holes are merging, they are orbiting around each other and gradually spiral closer together. You might expect that if they orbit fast enough, they will remain in orbit forever. However, the fast-moving black holes lose orbital energy by radiating away gravitational waves, which causes their orbits to decay. As they spiral toward each other, they orbit faster and faster. This causes the frequency of their gravitational wave signal to rise exponentially, which would resemble a chirping sound when graphed as a function of pitch. When the black holes finally collide, 3 times the mass of the Sun is converted into a deafening blast of gravitational waves, which races away from the collision site at the speed of light.

Before the discovery of GW150914, we had never observed black hole collisions directly, because black holes do not emit light. But after this event, LIGO has witnessed black hole mergers regularly across the universe, which could potentially solve the mystery of the oldest supermassive black holes. During the Dark Ages, stellar mass black holes and inter-mediate mass black holes could have merged repeatedly until they became supermassive. Additionally, supermassive black holes themselves could merge as well when they are brought together by galaxy collisions.

Some large galaxies have two supermassive black holes at their centers, which suggests that although galaxies merge, the final parsec problem may prevent the supermassive black holes from merging.

If supermassive black holes do indeed merge, we should observe a gravitational wave background consisting of emissions from mergers across the universe.

However, there is a problem. Based on our current observations, the largest black hole formed from mergers is the 142-solar-mass intermediate mass black hole discovered in 2020. And while we have already observed galaxies collide, we have never seen supermassive black holes collide.

When galaxies merge, their supermassive black holes gradually sink to the center of the new galaxy. As they orbit one another, they start to gravitationally disrupt nearby stars and fling them away from the core of the galaxy, which takes away some of their orbital energy. They also lose energy in the form of gravitational waves, which further decreases their separation.

However, when the supermassive black holes are 1 parsec (3.3 light years) apart, there is no longer enough space in which stars can orbit, so they cannot lose any more energy by ejecting stars. They would still lose energy by emitting gravitational waves, but the waves have such a low frequency that the loss of energy is tremendously slow. As a result, the black holes stall and cannot move closer together, at least for billions of years. This phenomenon is known as the *final parsec problem*.

In galaxy J1010+1413, located 2.5 billion light years away, scientists have observed two supermassive black holes that appear to be stalled. Each black hole has 800 million solar masses, and they were found to be roughly 430 parsecs (1,400 light years) away from each other, evidence that this binary pair is in a pre-merger stage. However, due to the final parsec problem, it is possible that they will never merge in the future.

Logically, supermassive black holes must have merged in the past, because galaxies merge repeatedly in order to grow. If the black holes did not merge, we would expect to see large groups of black holes near the cores of galaxies rather than one; but we don't find that. It is also the best explanation for how supermassive and ultramassive black holes grew to their current sizes. But with the final parsec problem in play, the way they can merge remains a mystery.

We do not yet know whether the final parsec problem is real or not. To prove or disprove the theory, we need to measure the gravitational wave signals emitted by the supermassive black holes as they spiral closer together. If this problem does not exist, which would mean that supermassive black holes can merge, we would expect to observe gravitational wave emissions from supermassive black hole mergers across the universe, which would all combine to form a *gravitational wave background*.

One possible analogy for the gravitational wave background would be a choir. Each singer's individual voice is unique, but their voices become indistinguishable from each other when they all sing the same note on the same beat. Likewise, if supermassive black holes frequently merge, they should all emit gravitational wave signals at the same time, which would blend together to form the gravitational wave background that we predict.

Gravitational waves from supermassive black hole mergers have the highest amplitude, so they appear far "louder" than gravitational waves from other sources like stellar mass black holes. But another important consideration is that the black holes start off in separate galaxies, and since they are initially very far apart, they would orbit each other incredibly slowly at first. As a result, the frequency of the gravitational waves they emit would be extremely low. This also means that the gravitational wave background created by supermassive black hole mergers only consists of low-frequency waves. Since the frequencies are outside the detection range of LIGO or other Earth-based observatories, we cannot detect the gravitational wave background using traditional methods.

One alternative method is to use the flashes of radiation from pulsars. Their pulses are so stable and regular that they could be used as incredibly precise clocks. However, passing gravitational waves stretch and compress spacetime, which increases or decreases the distance that the pulsar's light travels on its way to Earth, affecting the arrival times of the signals.

The North American Nanohertz Observatory for Gravitational Waves (NANOGrav) uses a network of pulsars called a pulsar timing array to detect gravitational waves from multiple sources. The team has measured the delays from 47 pulsars over a 13-year period and discovered something surprising: the low-frequency signal was the same in all of the pulsars at the same time. This observation is strongly indicative of the presence of the gravitational wave background, because in order to create a common low-frequency signal in all of the pulsars, they must be influenced by gravitational waves from different sources.

If confirmed, NANOGrav's finding will prove to us that supermassive black holes can indeed merge, and that there is no final parsec problem. Future space missions will also work to detect low-frequency gravitational waves. For example, the Laser Interferometer Space Antenna (LISA), scheduled for launch in 2034, will consist of a network of three interferometry satellites that are all equidistant from each other. Because the three satellites will be spread much farther apart than LIGO's two detectors and will experience little to no environmental disturbances, LISA will have a far wider detection range and will be able to observe supermassive black hole mergers more effectively.

The distinct strands of gas in NGC 6240 suggest that three galaxies, and therefore three supermassive black holes, are in the middle of a merger.

While NANOGrav's observations make it increasingly likely that supermassive black holes can merge, some scientists have proposed potential solutions to the final parsec problem. One intriguing theory states that two supermassive black holes can merge when a third black hole comes into the picture. This is possible, because three galaxies can merge all at once, bringing three supermassive black holes to the core of the new galaxy.

In late 2019, this idea was tested. In the Ophiuchus constellation lies a bizarre galaxy named NGC 6240. This galaxy, 400 million light years away, appears to be the remnant of a galaxy merger, containing huge tails of gas that span 300,000 light years. Astronomers initially believed that there were two supermassive black holes in the galaxy's heart, but when they examined the core in detail, they discovered that, in fact, there is a third supermassive black hole in this region as well, implying that a three-way galaxy merger had taken place.

Each of the black holes has roughly 90 million solar masses. Initially, the third supermassive black hole was hard to detect, because all three black holes orbit in a space less than 3,000 light years wide, which would make them difficult to distinguish from each other. Additionally, two of the black holes are active, so they appear brighter than the third, which is somewhat farther away from the other two. But with the high-resolution images of NGC 6240, we now have direct evidence that three supermassive black holes can merge together.

The third black hole could help the other two overcome the final parsec problem. When the first two galaxies merge, their supermassive black holes lose orbital energy by throwing away stars and gradually drift toward the core of the galaxy. The third galaxy later collides with the remnant galaxy, and its supermassive black hole also reaches the galactic nucleus. When the third black hole passes by the galaxy's center, it transfers more orbital energy away from the two stalled black holes, enough for them to finally collide. As they merge, the third supermassive black hole gets farther away from the merging pair, which we have seen in the images.

Based on NANOGrav's potential detection of the gravitational wave background, as well as NGC 6240's three supermassive black holes, it is becoming increasingly likely that supermassive black holes can merge. However, our current evidence is only indirect. The only way we will know for sure whether giant black holes merge is by witnessing a merger as it happens. If we do, it will solve a long-standing mystery. But when these monster black holes finally collide and gorge on material left over from the galaxy merger, they can create the most powerful light show in the universe.

Quasar jets, which are driven by the magnetic fields around the supermassive black hole, can cause mass destruction over millions of light years.

Galactic Powerhouses

The observable universe hosts trillions of galaxies. They can have a wide variety of shapes, sizes, and colors. We know that they all drift through space within the cosmic web, a vast complex held together by dark matter, and that they sometimes collide. However, galaxies are also classified based on their phase. Most galaxies, including our own, are calm, but active ones can be ablaze with light and can be seen clear across the universe.

In the 1960s, scientists discovered a bright object designated 3C 273. From Earth, it looks just like an ordinary star. However, spectroscopic studies of this object reveal that it has a substantial redshift, which means that its light is being stretched to longer wavelengths and losing energy as it travels through space. Since space is expanding, a redshift in the light of a distant object suggests that the object is moving away from us, and the higher the redshift, the farther away the object must be.

In the case of 3C 273, the redshift in its light suggests that it is over 2.4 billion light years away. Additionally, due to its redshift, most of the light on its spectrum is in the form of radio waves. Normally, individual stars cannot be seen from such a distance or emit such high quantities of radio light, so scientists could conclude that this was a different object entirely. It was classified as a quasi-stellar object (quasar for short), but at the time, no one knew what it was.

Other such objects were studied in detail using X-ray and gamma ray observatories, and scientists eventually came to the consensus that quasars are powered by actively feeding supermassive black holes at the centers of galaxies. We typically observe black-holes feeding for only a short amount of time, because they consume a relatively small amount of material during feeding events. However, quasars are fueled by galaxy-sized quantities of matter, which are constantly replenished from the surroundings. As a result, they can last for millions of years and affect their host galaxy much more profoundly.

The extreme luminosity of a quasar is determined by the immense energies in the super-massive black hole's accretion disk. The faster the disk orbits, the hotter and brighter it gets, and the stronger the magnetic fields become. If there is a powerful corona above the poles of the disk, energy stored in the black hole's magnetic fields can be accelerated to form jets, which blast away at close to the speed of light.

For decades, we have observed thousands of different quasars and studied their effects on their environment, but we do not definitively know what causes them. Then, in 2018, scientists found a potential answer when they studied a distant galaxy named W2246-0526. Spectra of this galaxy suggest that it is over 12.4 billion light years away, so its light has taken 12.4 billion years to reach us. Over that time, as the universe expands, its light undergoes a significant redshift, making it hard to study in detail. However, long-exposure images from the Atacama Large Millimeter Array (ALMA) suggest that a quasar may soon be born in this galaxy.

W2246-0526 is the most luminous galaxy we know of, shining 350 trillion times brighter than the Sun. Because of its unique spectrum, it is classified as a hot, dust-obscured galaxy (Hot DOG). The supermassive black hole at the core of this galaxy, which has 4 billion solar masses, is likely feeding, which generates light and heats the surrounding material. However, the galactic nucleus is shrouded in dust, which blocks most of the light. As a result, most of the light emitted from this galaxy is infrared radiation, which we detect as heat.

In November 2018, astronomers studying W2246-0526 found that it is currently merging with three other galaxies at once. ALMA images have found long strands of material protruding from the smaller galaxies, which implies that the collisions are not head-on. Instead, the smaller galaxies are likely in orbit around W2246-0526 and the large galaxy is gravitationally stealing material from its smaller neighbors. This gas would replenish the gas consumed by the supermassive blak hole, allowing the cycle to sustain itself for millions of years.

Eventually, when the four galaxies finally merge together, their supermassive black holes could merge as well. The black holes drag gas with them as they merge, increasing their food supply enough to potentially ignite a quasar. Upon formation, the quasar would radiate away high-energy light, drive black hole winds, and if the system has enough mag-netic energy, create jets. However, in some cases, the jets from a quasar are pointed directly at us, significantly changing the light signatures that we see.

Although quasars can violently damage a galaxy while active, they ensure that the galaxy maintains a healthy rate of star formation over the long term.

In 2019, scientists discovered a bizarre object named PSO J0309+27, located 12.8 billion light years from Earth. It is classified as a *blazar,* a subcategory of quasars whose light travels directly toward us. Unlike regular quasars, blazars only form with jets and emit light of all wavelengths, from gamma rays to radio waves. Additionally, blazars are far more energetic, but their light emission can vary over time, while quasars emit a steady flow of light. This is because when the jets travel directly toward us, we can measure the pulsations of the individual knots within them, and when they travel in a different direction, they appear to be a single structure.

Quasars were quite common in the early universe, but based on our observations, blazars were much rarer at this time. However, spectral analysis of PSO J0309+27 could potentially explain why. Scientists observed that in the closest vicinity of the supermassive black hole, the radio emission was strongest. Its jets, which travel 1,600 light years away from the black hole, are brightest in X-rays. Importantly, these measurements are consistent with predictions of the spectra of other high-redshift blazars. If PSO J0309+27 is like most other high-redshift blazars, and we have observed few others, blazars would indeed be rare in the early universe.

Since quasars and blazars are powered by actively feeding supermassive black holes, they can completely devastate their host galaxies. The high-energy light drives powerful quasar winds, which blow vital gas away and suppress star formation. Additionally, quasar jets, which can produce as much energy than trillions of stars combined, propagate across millions of light years, tearing massive voids in galactic gas clouds. Even when the jets strike the intergalactic medium, the energized gas blows away, reducing the supply of gas that the galaxy can obtain from outside. As a result, star formation is shut off and can be halted for millions of years.

However, astronomers are now starting to discover that quasars may have a creative side, and that they could be essential to ensuring the health of a galaxy. A galaxy must produce stars in order to live, but too many stars forming at once can actually be detrimental. Not only does the galaxy's gas supply get used up more quickly, but turbulence from star formation can prevent the remaining gas clouds from collapsing to form stars, reducing the lifespan of the galaxy.

With quasars in the picture, galaxies can easily mature. When the galaxy first forms, stars are forming at a high rate. However, the gas used to form stars also falls towards the supermassive black hole at the galaxy's core, which forms a quasar, halting star formation and blowing gas outward. Eventually, the gas at the center of the galaxy is completely used up, so the quasar turns off. Star formation resumes and could potentially be boosted by the gas pushed outward by the quasar's jets and winds. However, the cooling gas also sinks back toward the galactic nucleus and could re-ignite the quasar, starting the cycle over again.

As a result of intermittent periods of quasar activity, star formation rates fluctuate and reduces the rate at which the gas in the galaxy is used up. This ensures that the galaxy will live a long, protractive life. But if it wasn't for the supermassive black holes that drive quasars, galaxies would not be able to sustain star formation long enough for solar systems and life to evolve. Therefore, we owe our existence to them.

Although black holes big and small shape the universe around them in such profound ways, such as by shaping nebulae or driving quasars, the question of what lies inside them is perhaps the biggest unsolved mystery in modern physics. However, with the application of general relativity, we can start to piece it together, and the best place to start is the event horizon, the boundary between the known and unknown.

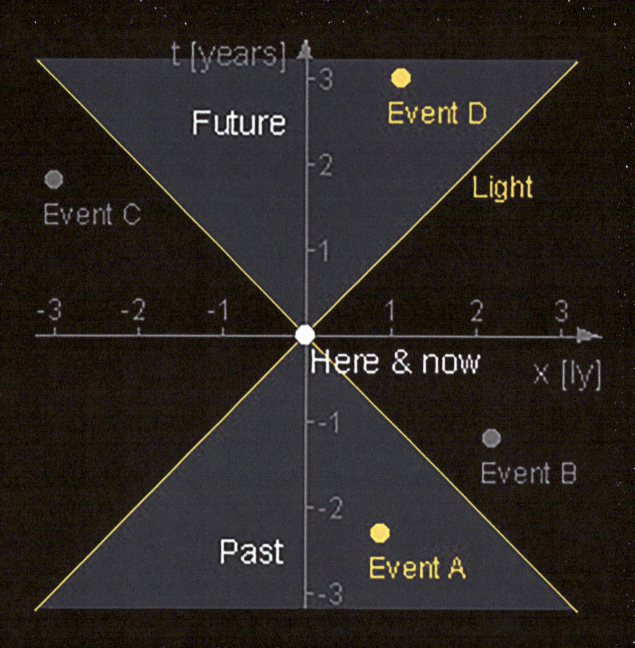

The observer can only follow trajectories in their future light cone or observe events in their past light cone, no matter where they are in space or time.

The Event Horizon

The first thing you might think of when we talk about black holes is the event horizon, their most seemingly obvious feature. Although it is commonly described as "the point of no return", it is scientifically defined as "the boundary beyond which events cannot affect an outside observer". However, the escape velocity below the horizon is greater than the speed of light, meaning that no matter or radiation can escape from inside.

As a result, light moving away from the center of the black hole can never reach the event horizon. Due to gravitational time dilation, an object approaching the event horizon from outside would have the same effect. An observer would notice the object move slower and slower as it got deeper into the black hole's gravitational field. At the event horizon, where the escape velocity equals the speed of light, time stops moving, so the object would appear to freeze and never quite cross the horizon. Additionally, the gravity of the black hole stretches the light from the object, creating a redshift. The object would have a higher and higher redshift and appear to completely fade away as it crosses the event horizon.

The optical phenomena an observer witnesses when the object crosses the event horizon may seem completely abstract. However, using mathematics, we can more clearly understand how it works, as well as what happens on the inside of the black hole.

Suppose we start with an x-y coordinate system. The x-axis represents distance, in light years, while the y-axis represents time, in years. Light travels along 45-degree lines, and vertical lines represent stationary objects. The observer is always at y=0, which is the present time.

Since nothing can travel faster than light, the line that models the path of an object cannot have a slope between -1 and 1. Therefore, we can trace out all the points on 45-degree lines that move away from the observer. This is the observer's *future light cone,* and it describes all possible paths the observer can take in the future. Likewise, the *past light cone,* which is formed from 45-degree lines below the x-axis, describes all possible trajectories in the past that could lead to the observer's current position.

If we were to plot a black hole on a spacetime diagram, its center, known as the *singularity,* exists at x=0, and its event horizon exists at a positive distance from the y-axis. However, it exists at all possible times (all real y-values). Light travels on 45-degree paths in flat space-time; but in the vicinity of the black hole, the path of the light can be curved so that they follow paths between 45 and 90 degrees. As a result, the light reaches the observer later than they would expect, creating the bright arcs and halos that we typically observe around black holes.

Now imagine a moving spaceship plotted on the spacetime diagram. In flat spacetime, its past and future light cones open 90 degrees in front of or behind them. However, as it gets closer to the black hole's event horizon, its future light cone slowly bends towards the black hole. This is because as gravity increases, the escape velocity increases, so the number of possible trajectories the ship can take to escape decreases. At the event horizon, where the escape velocity is the speed of light, there are no possible trajectories that lead away, and below the event horizon, all the ship's possible trajectories lead towards the singularity.

However, using a 2-dimensional spacetime diagram is not the most complete way of modeling an object's path, because as spacetime gets warped, the object's path curves, and its light cone can either stretch or contract. As a result, it becomes harder to restrict the possible trajectories leading toward or away from the observer. The solution is to use a diagram that includes infinite space and infinite time: the Penrose diagram:

The Penrose diagram compresses the lines of constant space and constant time such that they extend to all possible locations in one dimension of space or moments in time, but they all converge at the corners of the graph, known as conformal infinities. The horizontal edges represent space-like infinities, or infinite distances in space, while the vertical edges are time-like infinities, which describe the infinite past or infinite future. The diagonal edges of the diagram represent the past and future cosmic horizons, at which or beyond which light can never reach us.

Since the gridlines are compactified, light *always* travels along 45-degree paths, so an object's light cones always have a vertical orientation. Additionally, since the diagram only includes one dimension of space, any sideways motion brings the observer closer to the black hole. Therefore, the diagram can be used to model the paths of objects much more effectively, and understand what happens at the event horizon.

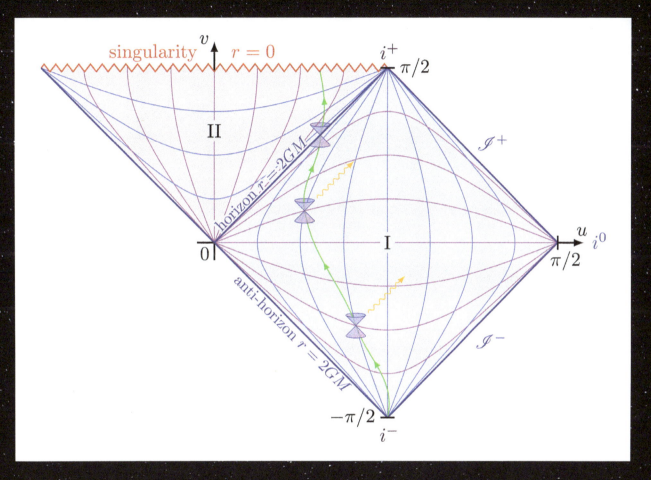

As shown on the Penrose diagram, when the traveler crosses the event horizon, their light only reaches the observer infinitely far in the observer's future.

The simplest Penrose diagram models flat spacetime, with space-like and time-like infinities. However, when we plot a black hole on the diagram, the future cosmic horizon on the graph is replaced by the black hole's event horizon. Towards the edges of the diagram, the gridlines are much closer together due to compactification, which models the curvature of spacetime just outside the event horizon.

Imagine the spaceship starting at the center of the diagram and moving towards the event horizon. The ship emits a regular light signal, but an observer would notice that the arrival times of the ship's signal get increasingly delayed over time as the ship gets deeper into the gravitational well of the black hole. At the event horizon, the ship's light signal moves at the speed of light against a lightspeed flow of spacetime. As a result, the signal emitted from the event horizon never reaches the observer, and the observer perceives the ship to be frozen at the event horizon forever.

From the perspective of a traveler aboard the ship, the view would be completely different. The traveler can only observe parts of the outside universe that are within their past light cone. As the ship gets closer to the event horizon, the portion of its light cone that includes the light coming from the outside universe gets smaller and smaller. As a result, the traveler's view of the universe is compressed into a circle that shrinks over time and eventually disappears as they cross the event horizon. Furthermore, due to gravitational time dilation, they would witness the future history of the universe in fast forward, and just as they crossed the event horizon, all of time would pass.

Once inside the event horizon, the flow of spacetime towards the core of the black hole is faster than the speed of light, meaning that the ship, or anything else that enters, will inevitably reach the singularity. On the Penrose diagram, this is shown by the fact that the object's future light cone only includes the singularity if it crosses the event horizon. This may mean that black holes should keep growing forever as they absorb more matter, but when quantum mechanics comes into the picture, everything changes.

Fundamentally, black holes are predicted and explained by general relativity, which explains the motions of large objects in our universe and how these objects interact with space and time as they move. However, the universe must also obey the laws of quantum mechanics, which explain the realm of subatomic particles. These two theories conflict at the event horizon, creating a problem known as the *black hole information paradox*.

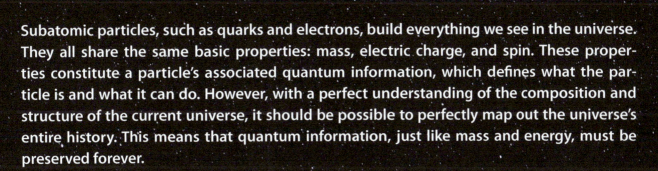

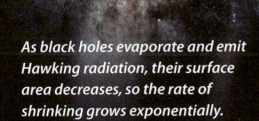

As black holes evaporate and emit Hawking radiation, their surface area decreases, so the rate of shrinking grows exponentially.

Subatomic particles, such as quarks and electrons, build everything we see in the universe. They all share the same basic properties: mass, electric charge, and spin. These properties constitute a particle's associated quantum information, which defines what the particle is and what it can do. However, with a perfect understanding of the composition and structure of the current universe, it should be possible to perfectly map out the universe's entire history. This means that quantum information, just like mass and energy, must be preserved forever.

As black holes gain mass and grow, they also accumulate quantum information. Although information cannot be destroyed, it does not have to exist only in parts of the universe accessible to us. Instead, the information that enters the black hole simply continues to exist inside the black hole.

However, in the 1970s, physicist Stephen Hawking predicted that black holes slowly evaporate and emit heat known as *Hawking radiation,* which is created by the black hole's distortion of the surrounding quantum fields. These distortions cause particles to flow away from the event horizon, and the energy used to create them must come from the mass of the black hole itself. As a result, the emitted thermal energy causes the black hole to shrink.

Hawking radiation produced by the evaporating black hole is perfectly random thermal energy, meaning that it does not hold any information, so when the black hole completely vanishes, there would be no way to know what fell into it in the first place. With less information, it would not be possible to predict the future history of the universe completely accurately. This violates the law of conservation of information, which ensures that all moments in the universe's history can be perfectly understood.

To this day, we do not know of a solution to the information paradox. However, scientists have thought about several ways that the information that fell into the black hole could be preserved. Perhaps the most feasible theory begins with considering the information from two different points of view: the traveler entering the black hole, and an outside observer. From the point of view of the traveler, they simply cross the event horizon and enter the black hole, and their information gets trapped inside.

However, we must also consider the perspective of the outside observer. From their perspective, the traveler gradually slows down as they approach the event horizon, and due to gravitational time dilation, they appear to freeze in time at the horizon. Since the observer can still see the traveler's light signal, it is possible that the traveler's information does leave the event horizon along with Hawking radiation.

According to black hole complementarity, although the traveler perceives their information to stay in the black hole, the observer perceives the information to leak away in Hawking radiation.

Although information cannot be destroyed, it cannot be duplicated either. If the traveler perceives their information to be inside the black hole, while the observer perceives the same information to exist on the outside, it may seem like there exist two copies of the information, which would violate conservation of information. However, the idea of *black hole complementarity* suggests a workaround.

Nothing can escape from inside the event horizon, so the observer, who is in the outside universe, can never access information from inside the black hole. Since time stops at the event horizon due to gravitational time dilation, the interior of the black hole exists on a different timeline than the outside universe. Therefore, the traveler can never access information from outside the black hole. This means that the interior and exterior of the black hole cannot be understood simultaneously.

Both versions of the information are identical. However, since the event horizon permanently separates both sides of the black hole, any observer, whether inside or outside the black hole, can only access one version of the information at any one time, either the information inside or the information outside. As a result, we can say that the observer and the traveler are looking at the same information, just from two different (complementary) perspectives, so the information would not be duplicated.

The traveler would easily be able to access their information inside the event horizon. However, there was initially no known way for the observer to detect the complementary version of the information, which should stay at the event horizon. Eventually, physicist Gerard 't Hooft proposed that an infalling object would distort the event horizon and create a dimple at the point of crossing, where the information is stored. Hawking radiation flowing away from the black hole carries the information away from the event horizon, at which point the observer can access it.

Black hole complementarity does have its drawbacks, which stem from quantum entanglement. When a series of quantum particles are correlated such that they share a unified quantum state, we say that the particles are entangled. For Hawking radiation to carry away information, the particles that create it must be entangled with each other and with all past Hawking radiation. However, this also suggests that the information must be entangled with past versions of the information. As a result, the black hole sheds information faster than we would expect, and it loses all its information before evaporating completely. In order to completely vanish, the black hole would have to lose past information, which is entangled with information from the present. Once again, the evaporation of the black hole violates conservation of information, meaning that black hole complementarity is not the answer.

The traveler's ship would be fried upon contact with the firewall, and the entanglements from their information would break, replenishing the firewall's energies.

With black hole complementarity unable to solve the problem, you might think that we may never figure it out. However, complementarity does pave the way for our best solution yet: the black hole firewall.

According to the theory, the entanglements of the information and Hawking radiation must be broken. If the particles are no longer entangled, the black hole loses less information as it evaporates, since past information is not lost. As a result, all the information is conserved, and the paradox is solved.

However, the process has an important consequence. Breaking an entanglement releases energy, just as breaking a molecular bond between atoms releases energy. When all the entanglements of the information are broken, the liberated energy builds up at the event horizon.

Since it exists right at the event horizon, the firewall is invisible to the observer, because light cannot escape. But the firewall transforms the event horizon into an impenetrable sphere of extreme energies that would burn the traveler's ship to a crisp. While the black hole would still gain mass, the traveler's information would stay at the event horizon and be carried away by Hawking radiation. Additionally, the firewall is self-sustaining, since its energies break the entanglements of the traveler's information, which releases more energy.

For now, the firewall is our best bet to solve the information paradox. But even it has its flaws. As predicted by general relativity, the event horizon is nothing more than a mathematical construct, the distance from the center of the black hole where the escape velocity is the speed of light. Normally, the traveler should not notice a single difference when they pass through. However, because of the firewall, the event horizon does become a distinct boundary between the inside and outside of the black hole, which violates our understanding of the fundamental definition of the event horizon. As a result, even the firewall is not completely effective.

We do not know whether the firewall exists or not, but either way, the only way to truly solve the information paradox is to unite general relativity and quantum mechanics into a single theory. And no one has managed to create a working theory of quantum gravity. As a result, the information paradox remains one of the biggest problems in modern physics, and many questions about our universe remain unanswered. But the hunt for a theory of quantum gravity, and hopefully a true solution, continues.

However, even if the paradox is solved one day, it would only explain what happens at the event horizon. Whatever exists inside the black hole remains a huge mystery and could be stranger than we could ever imagine.

$$\Delta s^2 = \Delta x^2 - c^2 \Delta t^2$$

The spacetime interval must always decrease over time, because the time parameter is negative, and time can only tick forward (t can only increase).

An Unknown Realm

Beyond the event horizon of the black hole lies the unknown. Since nothing can escape from the interior of the black hole, we can't know for sure what happens. All we can do is use the math of general relativity to make predictions.

The observer would see the traveler slow down and eventually stop as they cross the horizon, and their light signal would gradually fade until they became invisible. If the firewall exists, the traveler's ship would burn up, but if not, they would enter the black hole unharmed.

Inside the black hole, the traveler would not notice anything different with their immediate surroundings. However, the spacetime environment inside becomes so bizarre that the traveler would perceive time and space to switch roles. To understand how, we need to understand causality and the fundamental behaviors of space and time.

Space can be traveled in any direction. The directions up, down, left, right, forwards, and backwards are indistinguishable from each other, because they can vary depending on the observer's perspective. On the contrary, time is unidirectional, only moving from past to future. It can never reverse direction or stop moving.

Causality can be simply defined as the logical flow of cause and effect, and it is governed by the spacetime interval, which is defined by the equation $\Delta s^2 = \Delta x^2 - c^2 \Delta t^2$. The variable x describes distance in space, while t describes progression through time. The spacetime interval, s^2, is always the same for a sequence of events, regardless of where an observer is in space or time, because any combination of possible positions in space and time relative to the events will always yield the same value of s^2.

Since time only flows forward, the value of t in the equation always increases, because this maintains the proper causal flow. If an object is stationary, it does not move through space, but it still moves forward in time. As a result, its x parameter is constant, but since t always increases and the t parameter is negative in flat spacetime, its t parameter, and therefore its overall s^2 value, will decrease. This means that an object's spacetime interval can only decrease in forward temporal evolution.

You might think that since the equation consists of s^2, it would not be possible to have a negative spacetime interval, because we cannot take the square root of a negative number. However, physicists designate s^2 as a distinct quantity rather than the square of a number. As a result, the sign of s^2 only describes how far apart two events are in space or in time. If s^2 is positive, the events are farther apart in time than in space, so the interval describes a sequence of events that are in roughly the same location, but at distinct moments in time. Likewise, if s^2 is negative, the events are farther apart in space than in time, meaning that they occur at roughly the same time, but at measurable distances from each other in space.

Since forward temporal evolution requires a negative spacetime interval, the t parameter can only either be negative or equal zero. If the parameter becomes positive, this means that t has to decrease over time, and due to relative velocity time dilation, the only way for this to be possible would be with faster-than-light travel, which cannot happen. However, when we incorporate the gravity of a black hole into the equation, things get even weirder.

The x and t parameters in the spacetime interval equation must be multiplied by a constant to account for gravitational time dilation. In flat spacetime, this constant is just 1. However, in the vicinity of a black hole, gravitational time dilation causes time to get slower closer to the event horizon. The equation then becomes $\Delta s^2 = (1/(1-r^s/r))\Delta r^2 - (1-r^s/r) c^2 \Delta t^2$.

The constant rs describes the radius of the black hole. The variable r replaces x, since it now describes the distance from the center of the black hole. If r is greater than r^s, the t parameter remains negative while the r parameter stays positive, which would maintain causality. However, below the event horizon, where r is less than r^s, the multipliers become negative, flipping the respective signs of the r and t parameters.

To maintain a constantly decreasing spacetime interval, spacetime below the event horizon must flow toward the center of the black hole faster than the speed of light.

Remember that the spacetime interval must have space (r) and time (t) parameters, one negative and one positive, in order to maintain causal flow. The positive parameter, which is usually the r parameter, describes a space-like entity, which can be traversed in any direction or be stationary. The negative parameter, usually t, describes a time-like entity, which has unidirectional motion. This is because the spacetime interval must always decrease, and only the time-like parameter can constantly change, because only time moves unidirectionally. The space-like parameter can be constant, because it is possible to not move through space at all. Therefore, even if the space-like parameter does not change, as long as the ever-changing time-like parameter is negative, the spacetime interval will constantly decrease, which would correctly maintain causal flow.

Inside the black hole, the r parameter becomes negative, while the t parameter becomes positive. There is still one negative parameter and one positive parameter, which means that causal progression is still possible. However, since the r parameter is now the negative term in the equation, space becomes a time-like entity. Likewise, the now-positive t parameter causes time to become space-like. The spacetime interval would still decrease, maintaining the correct causal flow, but space now behaves like time and time behaves like space.

However, although the r parameter now describes time-like motion, we have to understand that it cannot equal zero, or else the parameter would not constantly decrease. As a result, the spacetime interval would stop decreasing, which would break causality. To prevent this impossible scenario, Δr must be a positive nonzero value, which means that spacetime flows in towards the singularity. Since r gets smaller and smaller compared to r^s, the only way to yield a constantly decreasing parameter is if Δr is greater than c, which means that spacetime must fall inwards faster than the speed of light.

When a black hole is plotted on a Penrose diagram, the event horizon can be modeled by the diagonal edges on the top left and top right. Beyond this line is the interior of the black hole, where the lines of constant space and constant time are switched and the singularity is a horizontal line at the top, the same level as the infinite future in the outside universe. As the traveler approaches the black hole, more and more of their future light cone encompasses the singularity, but it would still be possible to escape if they were to travel close to the speed of light. Their past light cone not only includes light from the observer, but also the light just above the event horizon that has been traveling away from the black hole since far in the traveler's past.

At the horizon itself, the traveler's future light cone no longer includes the outside universe, and the only way to avoid inevitably reaching the singularity would be to accelerate away from the black hole at the speed of light, which would only keep them eternally at the horizon.

Inside a Schwarzschild black hole, spacetime flows toward the singularity faster than light, but in a Kerr black hole, this flow stops at the inner event horizon.

One thing that the traveler would notice as they passed the event horizon would be a full layer of light rays at the horizon itself. This light is frozen at the horizon because it moves away from the black hole at the same speed as it is being pulled downward.

Inside the black hole, the traveler's entire future light cone only includes the singularity, since spacetime would fall towards the center faster than light. Since space is now a time-like dimension, only traversable in one direction, attempting to resist the faster-than-light cascade of spacetime would only hasten their descent. Although the traveler may seem to travel in a particular direction in space, they are actually moving along a time-like path. Rather than being the point at the center of the black hole, the singularity is better described as a moment in the traveler's future, because they will inevitably reach it.

However, the traveler would witness something truly bizarre as they fall through the black hole: they observe light from different moments in the black hole's history. They may pass light rays which point away from the singularity and fail to resist the flow of spacetime. Although the traveler perceives the light to be traveling upwards from beneath them, the light was likely emitted farther away from the singularity, since it was swept downwards by infalling spacetime.

Likewise, the traveler's past light cone describes the light that could possibly reach them. Although their future light cone only includes the singularity inside the black hole, their past light cone may still encompass parts of the outside universe, so they may still notice light from outside the black hole. Since the light moves inwards at the speed of light through a superluminal flow of spacetime, the light would fall past the traveler.

Time has become a space-like dimension, meaning that different distances from the black hole represent different moments in time. Moments in the traveler's past are closer to the surface, but different moments in their future are radially closer to the singularity. But they also see light from different points in time. Light from the black hole's past appears to approach them from below, while light from the future comes from above them. As a result, the interior of a black hole becomes a sort of "museum" where the traveler falls towards the singularity while seeing light from different moments in the black hole's history.

However, the views of different moments in time are not the only weird phenomena the traveler would notice on their journey towards the heart of the black hole. Fundamentally, the event horizon is the point of no return, at the surface of a black hole. However, this is only true for a Schwarzschild black hole, which has no rotation and no electric charge. In other types of black holes, which can rotate or gain electric charge, a separate boundary known as the *inner event horizon* can form, which completely changes our conception of what a black hole is.

In a Schwarzschild black hole, the traveler would simply descend towards the singularity while viewing light from different points in time. However, in a Kerr black hole, everything changes. Due to the rotation of the black hole, the singularity is no longer a point, but rather a ring. Furthermore, the rotation compresses the poles of the black hole. But most importantly, the infalling spacetime is spun into a vortex that orbits the ring singularity faster than light. This motion forms the inner event horizon, where the faster-than-light flow of spacetime towards the singularity is halted.

Since the spacetime at the inner horizon spins faster than light, all light and matter that falls into a Kerr black hole would pile up there and be infinitely compressed, resulting in a burst of infinite energy. However, as the rotation speed of the black hole increases, more and more of the inward cascade of spacetime gets swept into the whirlpool, causing the inner horizon to expand. When the black hole's spin increases enough, the inner and outer horizons will merge and dissipate. All that remains is the singularity, but since it is not surrounded by an event horizon and a faster-than-light inward flow of spacetime, it is known as a *naked singularity*.

Space and time around a naked singularity maintain their normal roles, so it is possible for an observer to approach it and leave without inevitably touching it.

While Kerr black holes can lose their event horizons with a sufficiently fast rotation, another type of black hole can do so in a different way. This black hole, known as a *Reissner-Nordström black hole,* is one that does not rotate, but is rather electrically charged. Its singularity is still a point, since it has no rotation, but all infalling electric charge would build up at the singularity. The electric forces exert an outward pressure that counteracts the inward flow of spacetime and once again creates an inner event horizon, where all infalling material will collide and beyond which nothing can travel. As the black hole accumulates electric charge, its inner horizon grows until it touches the outer horizon, annihilating both and leaving behind a naked singularity.

As a result, every black hole has a limit to the amount of spin or charge they can gain before shedding their event horizon. This threshold is determined by how large the inner horizon can grow compared to the outer horizon. When the black hole's inner horizon reaches the critical size, it becomes what we call *extremal.* If an extremal black hole were to gain any more spin or charge, it would lose its event horizon and leave a naked singularity in its wake.

The mass of the black hole determines the maximum amount of spin or charge it can gain before becoming extremal. This is because a more massive black hole has more gravity, which means that more force from spin or charge is needed to counteract the inward flow of spacetime and form an inner horizon. As a result, the black hole would need to gain even more spin or charge before becoming extremal.

Another important factor in the formation of extremal black holes is Hawking radiation. Normally, Hawking radiation consists of elementary particles, but radiation from the largest black holes consists of mostly photons. This is because the energy from larger black holes is not sufficient to generate elementary particles. As a result, large black holes that have gained electric charge will not lose their charge as they evaporate. The outer event horizon will shrink until it reaches the size of the inner horizon, forming an extremal black hole. Kerr black holes cannot do this, because they lose their rotation *and* their mass as they evaporate.

However, even extremal black holes are not eternal. As long as there is an event horizon, the black hole will still emit Hawking radiation, causing it to shrink. Since the inner and outer event horizons of an extremal Reissner-Nordström black hole are as close to each other as possible, Hawking radiation is still emitted, albeit at an extremely slow rate. But eventually, it will lose its event horizon and leave behind a naked singularity, which holds all the original electric charge that the black hole had accumulated. If the event horizons of extremal black holes can disappear over long periods of time, this means that in the distant future, there may not exist black holes, but rather particles and energy from Hawking radiation and charged naked singularities.

But the cosmic censorship hypothesis throws a wrench in the works. It states that there must be some mechanism that prevents extremal black holes from gaining any more spin or charge, preventing the formation of naked singularities. In order to understand how this works, we need to understand how black holes can gain spin or charge.

Black holes can only become extremal if they gain spin or charge faster than they gain mass, because gaining mass increases their capacity for spin or charge.

Black holes can become extremal by simply consuming matter. Kerr black holes gain spin from orbiting objects, which transfer their angular momentum to the black hole. However, for an object to fall into the black hole, it must lose orbital energy, meaning that it will enter the black hole with less angular momentum than when it started. We must also consider that spacetime around a Kerr black hole experiences frame dragging, which means that an orbiting object would also be carried by the swirling motion of spacetime. As a result, it would orbit even faster than normal and would have to lose more angular momentum to fall into the black hole.

However, when a Kerr black hole becomes extremal, it has the maximum rotation speed. As a result, even if the infalling object loses all of its angular momentum, it would still orbit the black hole, but *only* due to the frame dragging of spacetime. Even if the object is not truly stalled above the event horizon, the black hole would not gain any angular momentum, since the object only had motion *with* space and no angular momentum *through* space. This means that no trajectory into an extremal Kerr black hole can add enough angular momentum to make it superextremal.

But there is a possible workaround. The object itself can be rotating, meaning that it has intrinsic angular momentum. As a result, even if the object is being dragged by the spin of the black hole and not moving through space, it can still spiral into the black hole and add the angular momentum of its own rotation, allowing the black hole to shed its event horizon - theoretically.

In the case of a Reissner-Nordström black hole, the mechanism is somewhat complicated. Realistically, a charged black hole would be immersed in an environment surrounded by other matter, such as the core of a galaxy, so it would quickly become neutral. This is because it would only attract particles with the opposite electric charge, and since it repels like charges, the charges would cancel out, yielding a neutral black hole. But it is still possible for a charged black hole to exist in a cosmic void, as gravitational waves from black hole mergers could push them away from the merger site and out into intergalactic space.

The isolated charged black hole could gain charge from a flow of subatomic particles, but its mass would also increase at the same rate as the charge, so it would never become extremal. However, since electrons have a very small amount of mass, but roughly the same amount of charge as protons or neutrons, consuming high quantities of electrons would allow the black hole to gain charge faster than it gains mass, allowing it to become extremal.

But even this mechanism would not work, because the electric fields of the charged particles consumed by the black hole build up in a single electric field, which stores all of the energy from the charges. Since mass and energy are complimentary entities, the energy in the electric field converts to mass, which is always enough to prevent the black hole from crossing the threshold and revealing a naked singularity.

The singularity is the point where spacetime is curved infinitely, making it infinitely small and infinitely dense.

As a result, all possible ways for an extremal black hole to vanish and leave a naked singularity are either flawed or unproven. These problems stem not from the relativistic phenomena created by the black hole, but rather from basic physics concepts. We do not yet know if cosmic censorship must be maintained, but the answer depends on whether the existence of naked singularities would violate our understanding of physics.

The inner event horizon makes the interior of a black hole even more violent, especially if the black hole becomes extremal. However, if the traveler were to enter a Schwarzschild black hole, which has no rotation or charge and therefore no inner horizon, they would eventually reach the singularity, the strangest entity the universe has to offer.

Fundamentally, the singularity is the infinitely small and infinitely dense point right at the center of the black hole. Although infinities are extremely rare in the universe, the singularity can be explained in very simple terms. Newton's law of gravity states that the gravitational force (F_g) between two objects is determined by their masses (m^1 and m^2) and the distance between their centers (r). It can be calculated using the equation $F_g = G (m^1 m^2)/r^2$, where G is the gravitational acceleration between the objects.

The r^2 quantity in the denominator means that the force will increase exponentially as the objects get closer to each other, but the situation becomes complicated when r=0. You might expect an r-value of 0 to make the equation undefined, but in reality, the gravitational force becomes infinite.

Normally, an object's mass is spread unevenly throughout its entire volume. For the object to exert any significant gravitational force, its mass must be the most concentrated at its center and less concentrated farther away. The more mass is packed at the object's center, the higher its gravitational force. This means that to have infinite gravitational force, *all* the object's mass must be concentrated at the center. Having all its mass in zero size results in infinite density.

From a relativistic perspective, the black hole's singularity becomes completely different. Using the modified spacetime interval equation, which accounts for gravitational time dilation, we can calculate the curvature of spacetime based on r, the distance from the center of the black hole. Additionally, by taking the square root of s^2, we can calculate the rate of the flow of proper time, the actual amount of time an object experiences along its path. At r=0, where the traveler is right at the center, the coefficient of the t parameter becomes infinity. As a result, the overall value of the spacetime interval becomes infinite, resulting in an infinitely strong gravitational attraction.

However, there is technically another singularity described in the equation. At the center of the black hole, the time-like parameter becomes infinite, while the space-like parameter is zero. At the event horizon, where $r=r^s$, the t parameter becomes zero, but the r parameter would also be zero, since the object is stalled there and not moving. As a result, the overall spacetime interval would become zero. This becomes a problem, because the spacetime interval tells us the flow of proper time. Since nothing that normally experiences the flow of time can ever have a spacetime interval of zero, an object can never spend time at the event horizon, where it would not experience time ($t=0$).

In order to maintain a nonzero spacetime interval, the object would have to have a nonzero Δr value, meaning that it would have to move in space. Since it is at the event horizon, this means moving closer to the center of the black hole. As a result, the object's proper time clock would keep ticking.

So, a black hole really has two singularities: the point at the center, which the traveler will inevitably reach, and the event horizon, which they will inevitably cross. What lies in store beyond the central singularity, which is the inevitable point at the core of a Schwarzschild black hole, is a mystery. In all likelihood, the traveler would meet their end. Their ship would be crushed by the infinitely strong gravity, resulting in a flare of infinite energy, absorbed into the infinitely tiny point at the heart of the black hole.

However, although this is the common narrative, new physics provides a potential alternative. It is possible that upon contact with the singularity, the traveler's journey continues – but somewhere else entirely.

Since white holes are time-reversed black holes, the light they give off is actually the light that fell into the black hole when viewed forwards in time.

Mysteries of Wormholes

At the singularity, the traveler's journey appears to be over. There is nothing left to see about the black hole. But new mathematics suggests that the singularity provides a gateway to faraway places.

The Penrose diagram effectively describes the path of objects through spacetime by compactifying the gridlines to encompass infinite time and distance, but it is simply a visual representation of the Schwarzschild metric ($\Delta s^2 = (1/(1-r\_s/r))\Delta r^2 - (1-r\_s/r)\ c^2\ \Delta t^2$), from which the spacetime interval equation is derived.

The equation describes an eternal black hole, which has always existed and can never gain or lose spin or charge. Logically, black holes can never be eternal, because the universe itself has only existed for a finite amount of time. But in theory, the eternal black hole is observable in both the infinite future and the infinite past. Since time normally flows toward the future, we only perceive the black hole to progress forwards in time. However, when viewing the past version of the eternal black hole, everything changes.

We have observed many fundamental symmetries in our universe. For example, there are positive and negative electric charges, as well as north and south magnetic poles. The time reversal of a black hole creates its polar opposite: a *white hole*. The newly created white hole is identical to the black hole, but all its properties, such as its absorption of matter and radiation, as well as the traveler's one-way trip inside the event horizon and their inevitable arrival at the singularity, become time reversed. Matter and radiation move outward from the white hole's singularity faster than light, starting at some point in the past. Space experiences a time-like flow away from the singularity, so objects can only exit the white hole, and nothing can ever enter. But this would only be possible if eternal black holes could exist, which is impossible, since the universe itself is a finite age.

However, even if eternal black holes existed, this type of white hole can never be observed. In a black hole, the event horizon and singularity are separated by finite distances and finite times, but due to gravitational time dilation, the light from an object crossing the event horizon only reaches the observer infinitely far in their future. Likewise, the white hole's singularity and event horizon are also separated by finite distances and time, but its event horizon is separated from the observer by infinite time. Since it is a time-reversed black hole, the light from the white hole would be emitted infinitely far in the observer's past, so it would take infinite time for the light from the white hole to reach the observer.

Despite the inability to observe the past white hole, it may be possible to build another kind of white hole by manipulating an existing black hole. The black hole, which moves forward in time, is an infinitely deep gravitational well on the fabric of spacetime, and space flows downward toward the singularity, carrying matter and radiation with it. When reversed in time, the black hole turns into a white hole, where space flows away from the singularity, upward and out onto the flat spacetime.

However, the biggest problem with creating a white hole in this way is that the black hole is running backward in time. According to the 2nd law of thermodynamics, the level of entropy, or disorder, in the universe must always increase. Since the increase in entropy coincides with the flow of time, it defines time as a unidirectional entity that only flows forwards. This is because at time zero, the Big Bang expanded from a singularity, an infinitely small, highly ordered speck of pure energy. As a result, entropy could only increase from there as time moved forward.

If a black hole were to reverse in time and turn into a white hole, its entropy would start to decrease, which would seemingly violate this law. But it is possible for entropy to decrease in one specific location, as long as the cumulative entropy of the whole universe is increasing. Therefore, a spontaneous dip in entropy could temporarily turn a black hole into a white hole, but it would instantly explode when time reverts to its forward flow.

While white holes are yet another interesting astrophysical object predicted by general relativity, they could potentially be put to intriguing use by opening a *wormhole*, a path through spacetime that could lead to parallel universes. In the hypothetical case of an eternal black hole, the Penrose diagram would include the eternal Schwarzschild black hole to the top left of our universe, with its mirror-reflected version, the white hole, to the bottom left. However, if our universe appears to the right of the black hole and white hole in this diagram, there must be an identical region of spacetime to their left, which would be a parallel universe.

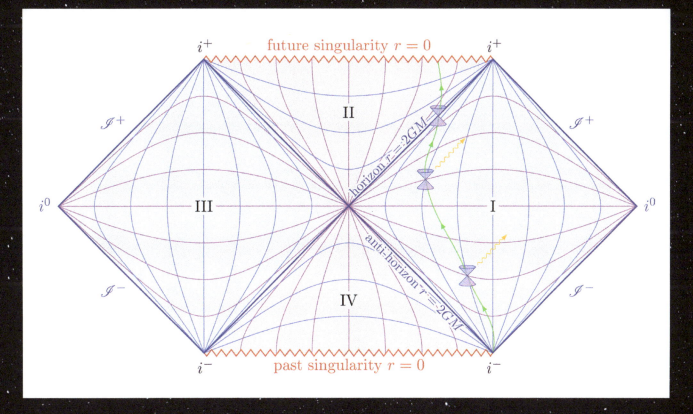

When the traveler exits the white hole (IV), although an observer in the first universe (I) may perceive them to move away from the white hole's event horizon, the traveler exits from the parallel event horizon into the parallel universe (III).

The wormhole to the parallel universe is untraversable, because the traveler's future light cone only includes the black hole's singularity once they are inside the event horizon. On the Penrose diagram, the traveler appears to be between two different event horizons, which could be crossed if they could travel faster than light. If they were to travel faster than light towards the event horizon they came through, they would exit the black hole into the original universe. However, if they were to travel faster than light deeper into the black hole, they would not reach the singularity faster, but rather exit through the parallel event horizon and into the parallel universe.

But even if the traveler could travel faster than light, there would only be a short period of time where they could use the Schwarzschild wormhole. Since space becomes time-like inside a black hole or white hole, different moments in time correspond to different layers of space at different distances from their singularities. At the white hole's singularity, both ends of the wormhole are cut off from each other. Over time, spacetime moves away from the white hole's singularity. Farther away from the singularity, the gravitational well is wider, so the throat of the wormhole becomes wider. The wormhole is at its maximum width exactly halfway between the white hole's singularity and the black hole's singularity. Since the past white hole and future black hole are time-reversal symmetric, moving into the future would bring the traveler deeper into the black hole's gravitational well, which would narrow the wormhole.

At both singularities, the two ends of the wormhole are completely disconnected. However, as time progresses away from the white hole's singularity and towards the black hole's singularity, the wormhole varies in width. From the white hole's singularity, the wormhole widens until the present time. Then it gets narrower until space reaches the black hole's singularity, at which point the ends of the wormhole will disconnect once again.

Since nothing can travel faster than light, Schwarzschild wormholes are unusable, and even if they could be traversed, they would only be open for a certain period. However, this only describes the wormhole created by a Schwarzschild black hole. Kerr black holes, which rotate, could create another type of wormhole that could be easier to use.

Remember that a Kerr black hole has an inner event horizon, which halts the inward flow of spacetime before it reaches the singularity. But if the traveler could pass through the inner horizon, they would find that the space and time in the region between the inner horizon and the singularity have returned to their normal roles. Since the black hole is rotating, the singularity has been spun into a ring, which, due to the rapid rotation rate, has developed an anti-gravitational force. However, if the traveler were to accelerate fast enough, they could pass through the ring. At this point, their journey would get even weirder.

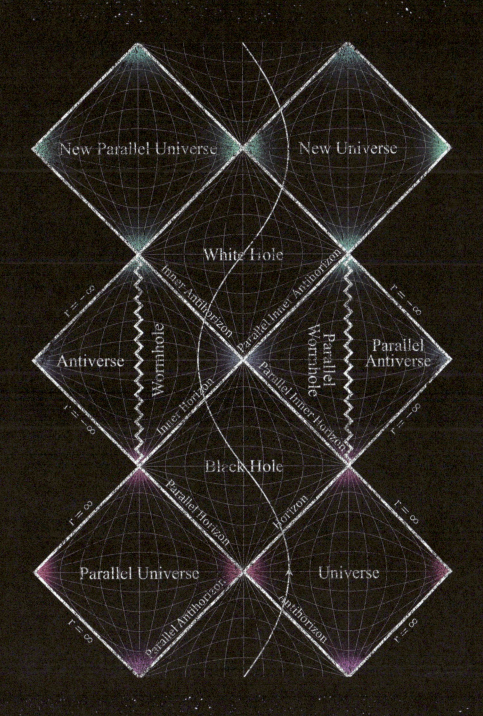

New Parallel Universe

New Universe

White Hole

$r = -\infty$

Inner Antihorizon

Parallel Inner Antihorizon

$r = -\infty$

Antiverse

Wormhole

Parallel
Wormhole

Parallel
Antiverse

$r = -\infty$

Inner Horizon

Parallel Inner Horizon

$r = -\infty$

Black Hole

$r = \infty$

Parallel Horizon

Horizon

$r = \infty$

Parallel Universe

Universe

$r = \infty$

Parallel Antihorizon

Antihorizon

$r = \infty$

The Penrose diagram predicts that the wormhole through a Kerr black hole links an infinite number of layers of parallel universes, with each layer existing on a different timeline.

The bizarre structure of the ring singularity creates a region where the traveler gets accelerated faster than light along a circular path through space. This means that they would also travel through time. However, since space has a circular path, the traveler's time would also move in a circle. This creates a *closed time-like curve*, which allows the traveler to loop through different moments in time by taking a looped path through space.

If the traveler were to travel the full circle, they would end at the same time they initially entered the ring. At this point, if they tried to exit the black hole, the repulsive force of the ring singularity would eject them past the inner event horizon. However, although they are passing through the same region of space, which they perceived as a black hole when they initially entered, the inward flow of spacetime from the outer event horizon to the inner horizon occurred in their past. This makes sense, because due to gravitational time dilation, the traveler would perceive the universe to experience infinite time as they crossed the outer event horizon into the black hole. The black hole and the original universe are both in the traveler's past light cone, and since their future light cone only points forward, they would have to travel outward. Since they are in a curved region of spacetime that resembles a black hole, but they would need to travel outward, they would exit the inner horizon into a white hole.

The eternal Schwarzschild black hole has a white hole only in its past. However, an eternal Kerr black hole has a white hole in its past and its future. Since the future white hole is a time-reflected version of the black hole, it would eject the traveler into an outside universe. But in the new universe, the traveler would perceive the original universe, the black hole, and the white hole to all be in their past. In the same location as the white hole was in the traveler's past, there would only be a black hole in their future, leaving no way to return to the original universe. However, if they were to enter this future black hole, they could take the same journey again, leading to yet another universe, which reveals the possibility of a multiverse.

Even if eternal black holes existed, the traveler could only reach these other universes if they could survive the inner event horizon of the first black hole, which is not possible. This means that although there may be other universes out there, we can never reach them. But another type of wormhole could be used to connect black holes and white holes in our own universe, allowing for instant interstellar or intergalactic travel.

Although the Einstein-Rosen wormhole would be the most feasible wormhole to use, a source of negative energy is needed to keep the two ends connected and widen the tunnel enough for a traveler to pass through.

To create an intra-universal wormhole, the black hole's singularity would be connected to the white hole's singularity, but on the same fabric of spacetime. Although the two points may be extremely far away from each other, this bridge in spacetime, scientifically known as the *Einstein-Rosen bridge*, brings the two points next to each other. As a result, the traveler could simply enter the black hole, cross the wormhole, and exit from the white hole.

Since wormholes connect two different points in spacetime, they would also allow for time travel. Initially, the two ends of the wormhole are at the same point in time, and their clocks are ticking forward at the same rate. But if the black hole was accelerated to the speed of light just after the traveler entered, its clock would stop moving due to relative velocity time dilation and remain at the same point in time when it was first accelerated. The white hole would continue moving through time. If the traveler were to reverse the wormhole and return through the second end, they would exit from the end that they started from, but since the first end was accelerated, it would not have moved through time. This means that the traveler would have visited another time period, but they returned at the same time that they left.

However, although this wormhole could be used to conveniently travel around the cosmos, it is not that simple. Since white holes can only be created temporarily, the wormhole would be incredibly unstable and collapse very quickly. A type of exotic matter was needed to hold the two ends of the wormhole together, and traditionally, this type of matter would have to have negative mass or negative energy. This matter would exert an outward force on the narrow spacetime near the singularities, which could keep the wormhole open. Although this type of matter could potentially hold wormholes open, it does not follow the mass-energy distribution requirements stated in general relativity.

While exotic matter may not exist, there could be potential alternatives for creating the negative energy needed to open wormholes. For example, scientists have observed that the expansion of the universe is accelerating, and have concluded that the acceleration is caused by a mysterious force known as *dark energy*, which is likely a form of repulsive energy that comes from spacetime itself. Since it causes spacetime to expand faster than normal, it could potentially be a force that can keep the throat of a wormhole open.

Another possible force is the *Casimir force*, which can create quantum fluctuations in the vacuum of space itself. If certain components of the quantum vacuum are blocked from a system, the system will gain a negative energy density. Although the negative energy density is small compared to the positive energy density of the surroundings, it could still add up to a sizable quantity if used on a large enough scale. In the case of a wormhole, the negative energy of the Casimir force could potentially keep the bridge wide enough open.

However, this negative energy would be in the traveler's way. For the traveler to safely pass through, the exotic matter would have to be arranged in a certain way along the path of spacetime, leaving enough space for the traveler to pass through.

These potential ways of holding the wormhole open could allow the traveler to use the power of the black hole to visit distant parts of our universe and different time periods, but it would only work if exotic matter actually exists, and these wormholes could only be used while the white hole stays stable. Many scientists still hope to find new types of exotic matter that can create the negative energy needed to hold open a wormhole. Perhaps in the future, we will have the technology needed to make wormhole travel successful, as well as learn more about black holes and white holes along the way.

A traveler entering a black hole may eventually reach a new universe, but only the traveler would know for sure.

The Future

From being central to galaxy evolution to opening the possibility of parallel universes or interstellar travel, the study of black holes is adding one vital detail after another to our picture of the cosmos. After the discovery of GW150914 and the image of M87*, black hole science has really turned into a scientific revolution.

However, for all we know and are learning every day, these perplexing objects still hold deep secrets that we have not uncovered - yet. We are currently developing new technologies that will be able to make more precise observations of black holes across the cosmos. New physics that can better explain them will soon come about, including a potential theory of quantum gravity, which would solve the information paradox.

Furthermore, our math can give us even more exciting prospects. For example, one idea suggests that the material that falls into the black hole builds up at the singularity, but if the black hole is connected to a white hole, the white hole's singularity would explode outwards, which could be perceived as another Big Bang. So black holes, in theory, could create new universes.

Another weird idea is that we are existing inside a black hole right now. To understand how, we need to think about singularities in terms of geodesics, which are defined as the straightest paths in a curved spacetime. They can be used to describe the curved trajectory of any moving object. Normally, they are defined for all moments in time, but they end at singularities.

The Big Bang theory predicts that all spacetime expanded from a singularity in the past, meaning that all geodesics in the universe merge there and end. A black hole's singularity is the endpoint of spacetime in the future, meaning that the geodesics in the black hole have a future endpoint at the black hole's singularity.

Based on the geometric descriptions of both singularities, the black hole's singularity and the Big Bang's singularity appear to be geometrically opposite. As a result, if entropy were to spontaneously dip and the black hole were to convert to a white hole, the white hole's singularity would match the behavior of the Big Bang's singularity. This could mean that our universe is on the other side of a black hole, and that there are new universes on the other side of black holes in our own universe. But this is all just theoretical based on our mathematics.

Either way, our fascination and curiosity, which make us human, are what lead to inquiry about such puzzling phenomena. Even if these interpretations of spacetime matrices are false, black holes have undoubtedly proven, and will continue to prove, to not be the sci-fi beasts they were long thought to be. Instead, they are the driving forces that allow stars, and therefore us, to exist. And they sometimes create cosmic fireworks, such as feeding events and quasars, which only add to the wonder our universe holds for us.

But we are just at the beginning of studying these objects. The more we learn, the more questions will arise, and the more it will motivate us to explore. This is the beauty of science and the existence of intelligent life in this cosmos: there is always something new to discover.

References

Abbott, R., T. D. Abbott, S. Abraham, F. Acernese, K. Ackley, C. Adams, R. X. Adhikari, et al. "GW190521: A Binary Black Hole Merger with a Total Mass of 150 M☉." *Physical Review Letters* 125, no. 10 (September 2, 2020). https://doi.org/10.1103/physrevlett.125.101102.

Britt, Robert Roy. "Milky Way's Central Structure Seen with Fresh Clarity." Space.com, August 16, 2005. https://www.space.com/1442-milky-ways-central-structure-fresh-clarity.html.

Byrd, Deborah. "A New Record for the Most Distant Quasar | Space | EarthSky." earthsky.org, January 13, 2021. https://earthsky.org/space/new-record-most-distant-quasar-black-hole-j0313-1806/.

Chandra X-Ray Observatory. "Famous Black Hole Has Jet Pushing Cosmic Speed Limit | ChandraBlog | Fresh Chandra News." chandra.harvard.edu, January 6, 2020. https://chandra.harvard.edu/blog/node/748.

Damond, Benningfield. "Windy Black Holes | StarDate Online." stardate.org, June 15, 2020. https://stardate.org/radio/program/2020-06-15.

Event Horizon Telescope. "Astronomers Image Magnetic Fields at the Edge of M87'S Black Hole." eventhorizontelescope.org, March 24, 2021. https://eventhorizontelescope.org/blog/astronomers-image-magnetic-fields-edge-m87s-black-hole.

Event Horizon Telescope. "Astronomers Reveal First Image of the Black Hole at the Heart of Our Galaxy." eventhorizontelescope.org, May 12, 2022. https://eventhorizontelescope. org/blog/astronomers-reveal-first-image-black-hole-heart-our-galaxy.

Harbaugh, Jennifer. "NASA's Chandra Finds Intriguing Member of Black Hole Family Tree." NASA, February 26, 2015. https://www.nasa.gov/mission_pages/chandra/intriguing-member-of-black-hole-family-tree.html.

Hille, Karl. "Collapsing Star Gives Birth to a Black Hole." NASA, 2011. https://www.nasa.gov/ feature/goddard/2017/collapsing-star-gives-birth-to-a-black-hole/.

Howell, Elizabeth. "'Winds' from Monster Black Holes Can Rapidly Change Their Temperature." Space.com, March 1, 2017. https://www.space.com/35881-black-hole-winds-quickly-change-temperature.html.

Jarman, Sam. "X-Ray Flares Spotted from behind a Black Hole." Physics World, August 10, 2021. https://physicsworld.com/a/x-ray-flares-spotted-from-behind-a-black-hole/.

Klesman, Alison. "Are These Supermassive Black Holes on a Collision Course?" Astronomy.com, July 12, 2019. https://astronomy.com/news/2019/07/ colliding-supermassive-black-holes.

Lazaro, Enrico de. "Astronomers Observe Bright Relativistic Jet from Distant Blazar | Sci-News.com." Breaking Science News | Sci-News.com, December 23, 2020. http://www. sci-news.com/astronomy/bright-relativistic-jet-distant-blazar-09182.html.

LIGO. "Gravitational Waves Detected 100 Years after Einstein's Prediction." LIGO Lab | Caltech, 2016. https://www.ligo.caltech.edu/news/ligo20160211.

Mohon, Lee. "Famous Black Hole Has Jet Pushing Cosmic Speed Limit." NASA, January 6, 2020. https://www.nasa.gov/mission_pages/chandra/images/famous-black-hole-has-jet-pushing-cosmic-speed-limit.html.

———. "The Recipe for Powerful Quasar Jets." NASA, October 14, 2020. https://www.nasa. gov/mission_pages/chandra/images/the-recipe-for-powerful-quasar-jets.html.

NANOGrav. "NANOGrav Finds Possible 'First Hints' of Low-Frequency Gravitational Wave Background." nanograv.org, n.d. http://nanograv.org/press/2021/01/11/12-Year-GW-Background.html.

NASA. "Black Hole Image Makes History; NASA Telescopes Coordinate Observation."
    NASA, 2019. https://www.nasa.gov/mission_pages/chandra/news/
    black-hole-image-makes-history.

NASA Jet Propulsion Laboratory (JPL). "The Most Luminous Galaxy Is Eating Its Neighbors."
    NASA Jet Propulsion Laboratory (JPL), November 15, 2018. https://www.jpl.nasa.gov/
    news/the-most-luminous-galaxy-is-eating-its-neighbors.

Neutelings, Izaak. "Penrose Diagrams of Minkowski and Schwarzschild Spacetime." TikZ.
    net, n.d. https://tikz.net/relativity_penrose_diagram/.

Nicholl, Matt. "An Outflow Powers the Optical Rise of the Nearby, Fast-Evolving Tidal
    Disruption Event AT2019qiz." academic.oup.com, October 12, 2020. https://academic.
    oup.com/mnras/article/499/1/482/592011142.

Nowakowski, Tomasz, and Phys.org. "Ultramassive Black Hole in NGC 1600 Investigated
    in Detail." phys.org, February 22, 2021. https://phys.org/news/2021-02-ultramassive-
    black-hole-ngc.html.

Pappas, Stephanie. "Magnetic Field around a Black Hole Mapped for the First Time."
    Scientific American, March 24, 2021. https://www.scientificamerican.com/article/
    magnetic-field-around-a-black-hole-mapped-for-the-first-time/.

PBS Space Time. "PBS Space Time | Dissolving an Event Horizon | Season 6 |
    Episode 21." www.pbs.org, June 30, 2020. https://www.pbs.org/video/
    dissolving-an-event-horizon-mmfqyk/.

———. "PBS Space Time | How Black Holes Spin Space Time | Season 6 |
    Episode 9." www.pbs.org, April 10, 2020. https://www.pbs.org/video/
    how-black-holes-spin-space-time-klqijt/.

———. "PBS Space Time | How Time Becomes Space inside a Black Hole | Season
    2 | Episode 42." www.pbs.org, March 29, 2017. https://www.pbs.org/video/
    how-time-becomes-space-inside-a-black-hole-qmyfsh/.

———. "PBS Space Time | Mapping the Multiverse | Season 6 | Episode 16." www.pbs.org,
    May 29, 2020. https://www.pbs.org/video/mapping-the-multiverse-ymock6/.

———. "PBS Space Time | the Black Hole Information Paradox | Season 4 | Episode 27." www.pbs.org, August 29, 2018. https://www.pbs.org/video/the-black-hole-information-paradox-wr2qmx/.

———. "PBS Space Time | What Happens at the Event Horizon? | Season 2 | Episode 28." www.pbs.org, December 8, 2016. https://www.pbs.org/video/what-happens-at-the-event-horizon-i5rxos/.

———. "PBS Space Time | What's on the Other Side of a Black Hole? | Season 6 | Episode 10." www.pbs.org, April 10, 2020. https://www.pbs.org/video/whats-on-the-other-side-of-a-black-hole-5hlra9/.

———. "PBS Space Time | White Holes | Season 3 | Episode 16." www.pbs.org, April 11, 2018. https://www.pbs.org/video/white-holes-7gg7ck/.

———. "PBS Space Time | Will Wormholes Allow Fast Interstellar Travel? | Season 6 | Episode 13." www.pbs.org, May 29, 2020. https://www.pbs.org/video/will-wormholes-allow-fast-interstellar-travel-swsxrf/.

Rutgers Physics. "The Faraday Effect." Rutgers University, n.d. http://www.physics.rutgers.edu/~eandrei/389/faraday.pdf.

Sci News. "Astronomers Find Three Supermassive Black Holes in NGC 6240 | Astronomy | Sci-News.com." Breaking Science News | Sci-News.com, November 22, 2019. http://www.sci-news.com/astronomy/three-supermassive-black-holes-ngc-6240-07832.html.

———. "Astronomers Monitor Flare from Nearby, Fast-Evolving Tidal Disruption Event | Astronomy | Sci-News.com." Breaking Science News | Sci-News.com, October 13, 2020. http://www.sci-news.com/astronomy/flare-nearby-fast-evolving-tidal-disruption-event-08944.html.

Specktor, Brandon. "Mysterious 'Fermi Bubbles' May Be the Result of Black Hole Indigestion 6 Million Years Ago." livescience.com, May 27, 2020. https://www.livescience.com/fermi-bubbles-black-hole-shock-wave.html.

Strickland, Ashley. "Astronomers Witness 'Spaghettification' of Star Shredded by a Black Hole." CNN, October 12, 2020. https://www.cnn.com/2020/10/12/world/star-spaghettification-black-hole-death-scn-trnd/index.html.

CPSIA information can be obtained
at www.ICGtesting.com
Printed in the USA
LVHW010930280523
748256LV00012B/1130

9 781039 149700